How to Settle Your Claim and Get the Money You Deserve!

A Guidebook for Property Insurance Claim Resolution

By Richard L. Carter Jr. B.S., M.A.

Licensed Public Adjuster

First Printing: 2015

ISBN 978-0-692-71443-0

Richard L. Carter Jr 23 Cub Drive, Thomasville, North Carolina 27360

www.Rick@howtosettleyourclaim.com. For author contact.

For book information and ordering visit: www.HowtoSettleYourClaim.com

Ordering Information:

Special discounts are available on quantity purchases by churches, corporations, associations, educators, and others. For details, contact the publisher at the above listed address.

U.S. trade bookstores and wholesalers: Please contact Richard L Carter Jr. email: Rick@howtosettleyourclaim.com

Dedication

To Julie, my wonderful wife. You are beautiful in every way.
The support and encouragement you have offered me is
without limits and I am truly grateful! To all my amazing children,
thank you all for your abounding love as we have
traveled together on this journey called life.
Your affection and belief in me brings me great joy!

Thanks to you, my very good friend,
Gary Pennington, Public Adjuster of
- San Antonio, TX, for
giving me a start in this business, and so freely sharing
your experience and knowledge.

A Few Recent Testimonials

"Rick Carter stepped in to help our family after we had experienced a fire, at a time when emotions were strained and our future looked bleak. Thanks to his help we have received well over $200,000 from our insurance company. Rick immediately began to prioritize what needed to be done and we felt a heavy load lift from our shoulders. He inspected our home, met with contractors, met with the insurance adjuster, reviewed and created estimates for repair, and met with our insurance company time after time to negotiate for more money on our behalf. Not only did Rick obtain funds for the cost of repairing our home, but he also led the way in helping us document all of the damages to our furniture, clothing, electronics and other contents. He has an exceptional team that assists him, and when the time came to hire contractors for the repair, Rick guided us as we made these selections. We are so grateful for the service that RL Carter has provided and heartily recommend their services."

~ Harold and Tammy M.

"We had an extensive fire in our two-story home and our insurance company sent out an "independent adjuster". They offered us $96,000.00 after much personal negotiation with a promise that there would be "no further payment or compensation, and we should take their offer."

"We consulted with Public Adjuster Rick Carter. His expertise and diligent repeated negotiations could improve our compensation to $175,000.00. I highly commend Rick for understanding and acquiring proper funding for our insurance claim."

~John W.

"We had water damage to our property. Rick reviewed our claim and Rick more than doubled the initial estimates for the claim. Rick has a great work ethic and is a man of character. I highly recommend RL Carter - Adjusters for the Insured."

~ Duvalle E.

"Rick Carter offers understanding and peace of mind to the average homeowner who may feel overwhelmed by filing an insurance claim. His insight makes the entire process seem simple and manageable. It would take years to learn all of the things that Rick makes available to get everything that you need to cover your insurance claim."

~ David O.

"In the fall of 2016 my brick house was damaged by a speeding car that struck the front of my home. An insurance company representative visited to assess the damage. This "senior" insurance representative submitted his observations and estimate of repair, and was about to issue payment.
Fortunately, I had been referred to public adjuster Rick Carter for assistance.

Upon review, Rick felt that I was being underpaid and was in disagreement with the offer from my insurance company. Another offer was then made by my insurance company, and again Rick refused the offer. I began to realize that Mr. Carter is an astute observer and evaluator of structural damages and is very knowledgeable of the cost for repairs.

I was greatly impressed by Mr. Carter's concern for my safety and welfare while living in a damaged home. I rate Mr. Carter's professional negotiation skills as a public adjuster and his concern for his clients a FIVE on a scale of 1-5. His diligent efforts on my behalf increased my compensation by 94% from the first offer made by my insurance provider."

~ Elizabeth A.

"We hired Rick to work our flood claim and I am certain that Rick got us total and fair replacement value and I wouldn't dream of managing a claim without a personal adjuster. I highly recommend Rick."

~ Doug K.

"After my kitchen caught fire I was concerned how I would get my home repaired as I had previously had a bad experience with my insurance company. The Fire Company estimated my damages at $3,000.00 After meeting Rick Carter, things turned around. Rick established a relationship with my insurance company, came out and estimated all my damages, met with my insurance adjuster and walked him through all the damages. Rick was thorough and was able to negotiate a quick settlement of over $27,000 Most of all, I was able to have the peace of mind knowing that I was in good hands."

~ Wanda W.

I have referred people to Rick Carter six times with absolutely fantastic results. Rick fights for the benefits of my customers as if they were family. His wealth of knowledge combined with hard work produced success each time I have referred him. I highly recommend R L Carter - Adjusters.

~ Scott C.

We highly recommend Rick Carter to anyone needing his public adjuster services. He is professional, trustworthy, knowledgeable, and has a key eye for details. His ability to identify undiscovered damage and needed repairs is amazing. You can trust his work and his word.

~ Michael C.

We had water damage to our house and wanted to make sure that we were being properly taken care of by the insurance company. We found Rick online and he came out the next day to look at the damage. He was very kind and professional, and took the time to explain what the insurance company was willing to pay for and what he thought we should be getting paid for. Even though he didn't take the claim, he took the time to help us ask for other things not included on the claim and gave recommendations for reconstruction. I would highly recommend him to anyone in this situation.
~Erin S.

A few recent claim successes not found in book.

The owners were devastated after the fire. Although they were paid enough for structure repair, after 11 months only $12,000 in contents had been paid. Using pictures from before and after the fire, we re-created the contents, determined the value and could negotiate a total payment to the owner of $197,000.

After a garage fire, we negotiated the rebuild, contents and living costs for over $250,000 in payment. We then aided in contractor selection. The owners are now back in their remodeled home.

Even though a plumbing leak had occurred in this home and insurance payment was already issued, we reviewed the damages and were able to increase the claim by more than 100%.

Hurricane Matthew flooded large portions of North Carolina. New Beginnings Church suffered a disastrous flood, with water in the building for three days. The church was expecting to receive $50-60k. We could negotiate a maximum policy limit settlement of $216,000.

A speeding car drove off the road and into this house. The insurance company made an offer. Not satisfied, we were then able to negotiate an increase of 94%, resulting in over $34,000 paid to the property owner.

After a plumbing leak, the insurance company offered the homeowners $14,000 for repairs. After being contacted, we examined the damages, wrote up a new scope of repair and re-met with the insurance company representative. We then settled the claim for more than $27,000.

A small home four bedroom home suffered a fire loss. We were able to negotiate the claim and obtained $137,000 for the structure and another $60,000 in policy limits for the contents. The owners are now building a new home.

Table of Contents

Addendum

1

This book is about...

This book is about techniques and common sense that the author has used successfully in helping property owners achieve greater financial results in the insurance property claim settling process.

This book is not about vilifying insurance companies. Insurance companies are an ingenious creation and help minimize the risks associated with a loss by sharing the risk with many policyholders. Without insurance companies and the policies that they write, the world would be a much gloomier place. Our modern world could not function without them.

Although comprehensive, this book is not exhaustive.

It is primarily intended for property owners of single family dwellings. This book speaks in terms of generalities. It cannot address specific issues in regard to your specific claim.

I am not a lawyer and this book is not designed or intended to give legal counsel or advice. Your policy with your insurance company is a legal document. Although there are many similarities in policies, every and "yes, I mean every!" policy is different.

It is impossible for one book or source to have answers specific to your legal contract (your policy) as they differ widely.

Regardless of what you may or may not do, there may sometimes be a claim that you just cannot settle on your own. Although there might be several reasons, this is especially true if the dispute is over coverage issues, that is, whether the loss is a covered loss.

If you are disputing coverage issues then you may need to get legal counsel from an attorney knowledgeable with property damage issues, your individual insurance policy, and the legal precedents which have been established in your own state. This book does not attempt to answer these questions.

The author assumes no liability for the information or results of this book. It is to be understood that your individual policy along with the provisions of your state are the ultimate authority. This book is merely a guide for claim resolution.

2

Introduction or "Why you need this book…"

This book is designed to take you step by step through the claims process and will give information and proven techniques so that you will know How to Settle Your Claim and Get the Money You Deserve.

If you are reading this book then it can be assumed that you, or someone that you know, has had an unfortunate event happen to your home or business property. The extent of your damage was sufficient for you to file or consider filing a claim with your insurance company. Most people have never filed a homeowner's, or property owner's claim, and do not know what to expect.

Many assume that the insurance company will simply "take care of it", only to find out later that things "did not go as they expected" and that the actions of their insurance company may not be sufficient to restore their property to its pre-existing conditioning. The outcome of your claim should NOT be left to chance, nor should your active participation in it be left for "sometime later if I'm unhappy". Don't wait to become active in your claim because it will limit your chances of success. Be knowledgeable! Knowledge is Power!

Although many people have had experience in filing a claim for a fender bender or with their medical insurance, there are some significant differences between these types of claims and a claim for property damage.

Auto claims are usually estimated by auto body professionals. Many insurance companies make it a practice to have the insured auto owner obtain two or three estimates from approved body shops. Indeed, some body shops can handle your claim with your insurance company minimizing your involvement. Body shops and mechanics with experience estimate the damages and are usually the very ones who will end up doing the work. The insurance company works with the auto body shop and or mechanic to restore your vehicle.

In a similar manner, with a health insurance claim many times the doctor's office or hospital files the claim's paper work directly with your insurance company. You, the insured, and the insurance company rely upon the expertise of physicians or medical equipment to correctly evaluate and diagnose your condition (damage). The expertise of these health professionals in most cases far exceeds the expertise of the insured and patient.

In the auto and health insurance examples, the insurance company relies upon the expertise of uninvolved, unsalaried personnel to determine the cause, extent of the problem and a prescription of what the cure will be. The people doing the diagnosing are in most cases the same ones who will fix the problem and the ones who will bill for their time.

Unfortunately, in a property claim the same method is usually not upheld. Instead of third party experts diagnosing the problem and prescribing a solution, most of the time insurance companies send out one of their own employees to diagnose, prepare a repair plan and estimate the cost.

Because of this, the dollar amount that you recover is often based upon the sole opinion of an adjuster that may or may not have estimated your damages properly. Although there are exceptions to this rule, this is generally the case. This is not to say that insurance adjusters are bad. There are many good ones and most try to be conscientious. Most have some level of training and insurance credentials. However, insurance adjusters are on the payroll of the insurance company and their first loyalty lies with their employer. To further complicate this issue, when a catastrophe hits a community such as a hurricane, flood, tornado or earthquake, insurance adjusters can be overworked and overwhelmed by the sheer number of claims which have been suddenly thrust upon them, making it difficult for them to take all the time necessary to evaluate your damages. It is particularly in these circumstances that some things will often be overlooked. In contrast, a Public Adjuster may devote him/her self to fewer claims while providing more in-depth attention to detail.

Therefore, it is prudent and necessary for you to be prepared. It is helpful to have a third party, someone not on the insurance company's payroll, examine the damages that your home or property has sustained. The best choice is to have someone, or a group of experts, who have an in-depth knowledge of construction methods, and costs relative to a given locale, someone familiar with insurance policies and their sometimes-complicated meanings, and someone experienced in settling claims with insurance companies. This book was written by someone that understands this process. With the knowledge that this book imparts, you will be better prepared and very likely find greater success in settling your claim.

The book is designed to educate you in the claims process from beginning to end, and ideally should be read in that order.

If you already in the process of your claim and have encountered some problems you might want to jump ahead to chapter 23 and 24 for some quick advice, then go back and read the book through.

If you are trying to decide if you should file a claim, then go to chapter 4 and read that first. Then go through the rest of the book. Then go back to chapter 11 "How to file your claim"

If you find the book a little tedious, or are presuming everything will "go well" with your claim, jump ahead to chapter 24. This will give you some clues as to what your claim future might hold if not dealt with properly to begin with. Then go back and read the book.

Chapters 15 and 16 provide examples of checklists to help document damages inside and outside your home or property, along with contents. Don't delay or overlook this very important part of your claim. Checklists can be found in the addendum at the end of book

Throughout the book reference will occasionally be made to "Public Adjuster" I suggest now you skip to chapter 19 and read "The Difference between and Insurance Adjuster and a Public Adjuster". Do this now, so you will understand the distinctions of the Public Adjuster and how their expertise can work for you. I am a Public Adjuster and consumer advocate.

Remember this book is a guideline to successful insurance claim resolution. The concepts in it have been proven through both failure and victorious experience. I trust you will benefit.

Please let me know how things work out for you and if you would like to, please review the book on line. Thanks!

With that being said, let's discover how to settle your claim and get the money you deserve.

3

Specific Types of Losses

Hurricane

A hurricane can bring massive damage to a large area. Some of the swaths of a hurricane may cut a section of damage 20 miles wide and across entire states. It is estimated that Hurricane Katrina brought damage to over 90,000 square miles. Damage from hurricanes can vary greatly from home to home. The design of the home and its location can greatly affect the impact of the storm. Homes that are located on barrier islands or close to the coast are the ones that are usually most impacted. For those on the coast there can be the added issue of storm surge. Heavy winds and torrential rains can cause severe water damage to homes.

Often in a hurricane strong gusts of winds can peel away roofs and or roofing materials, and soffits under the edge of roofs can be blown up as the force of the hurricane winds blow against the side of the property and cause an uplift of the roof.

Hurricanes cause additional stress because property owners may be asked to evacuate their property and leave their home unattended. During the storm and afterward, it is common to experience power outages as trees lose their limbs and knock down power lines. Items in the refrigerator and or freezer can go bad do the loss of power and can leak out over the kitchen floors.

Rising flood waters can also be a problem if a home is in a low-lying area it. If your home was flooded due to rising flood waters, then read the chapter on the flood loss. You may have to file two separate claims. Flood waters can be very destructive within the home. I have personally been in homes where flood waters came in from over the window sills as bayous were flooded. It can take a community many months or years to recover from a hurricane.

If your home was flooded from a hurricane there may be a dispute over coverage with your insurance company. This is especially true if you did not have flood insurance. Sometime hurricane victims will have a claim for flood damage and a separate windstorm or hurricane claim. You will have to review your policy for coverage and deductibles.

One of the issues of a hurricane can be the overwhelming demand it places upon insurance adjusters. This excessive demand can sometimes influence the amount of time they can devote to each claim. This may mean that some items of your claim may be overlooked. This is another important reason why you must complete your own damage checklist for the exterior and interior of your home. Your checklist list can help your adjuster and/or serve as a mirror to determine if things have been overlooked. So, be sure to do your homework!

Take as many pictures as possible of rooms and possessions. If your home has been demolished or moved from its foundation, then it should be totaled and your insurance company should probably pay you your policy limits.

You will have to review your policy for this information. Don't forget to file a claim for any other structures that you may have or had on your property. Review your policy to see what it says about additional structures, fences, trees, pool enclosures, debris removal, and so forth. You may also be entitled to loss of use coverage if the storm damage affects your business.

You know better than anyone else what you had in your home, and will need to make a list of contents. For success in this claim it is crucial to document the contents of your home. Take as many pictures as possible of rooms and possessions. If your home was not totaled, you will have to survey the damage closely. Use the content damage checklist. This will help your adjuster estimate the damage and serve as a mirror to check the adjuster's estimate.

Often, the severe winds related to a hurricane will damage a roof. Roof shingles may be blown away. If you have a clay tile or other type of tile roof, it is possible that the tiles have been uplifted. This weakens their attachment to the roof and they can be more easily blown off during the next windstorm. If you have a clay tile or barrel type of tile on your roof, be sure to have it thoroughly inspected by an experienced roofer. Hurricane force winds can have an uplifting effect on the tile. If they have been lifted, then nails or mortar securing them have been pulled loose. This compromises the roof's strength and lifespan. This type of roof could be loose, yet still not be leaking. It is important to try to minimize damage from rain by covering your roof or performing temporary repairs. This book has more information under "duties of insured after a loss".

You should have at least one roofing company come out and inspect your roof and give you a written estimate. If possible, have the roofer go up into the attic area to look for leaks and separation of roof trusses which may have occurred. Roof trusses can become loosened from the high winds and can weaken the structural integrity of

8

your home. Another place to look is at windows and doors. Do they rattle, or not close and open properly? Use the damage checklist to survey your home closely.

If any of the following appears, roof trusses, doors and windows that won't open or close, new-found cracks in walls, ceiling, or floor, then it is wise to consult with an engineer familiar with structural problems. In most cases it is well worth the money if he/she finds that your home has been damaged because of the storm. The engineer's report should be in writing and include a detailed plan of repair. A contractor can then write an estimate based upon the engineer's recommendations. Submit both reports to your insurance company. Remember, in most cases your adjuster is not an expert roofer, or an engineer. Carefully review this information and get the best experts possible. You will be glad that you did!

3b

Flood Loss

Normally, homeowner's insurance policies do not include flood insurance. There is a separate policy that is sold under the National Flood Insurance Program or NFIP. Although your agent may be the one who sold you your policy, it is a separate policy backed by this federal program. In 1968 Congress created the national flood insurance program.

If your property has flood insurance, make sure that you have enough coverage. If you purchased your home several years ago and the property value has increased, then make sure that you have increased your homeowner's and flood insurance policy limits to keep up with the increase of property value. If you are underinsured and your home is totaled or severely damaged, then you will not be able to replace it. Also, sometimes people pay off a mortgage and fail to maintain flood insurance. Perhaps there is no mortgage or you inherited your home. Make sure that you have this insurance if it is available. Don't get stuck without this coverage if flooding is a risk.

What to do immediately after a flood...

Use extreme caution and avoid disaster areas.

Take Pictures

Take pictures of the damage, both building and its contents, for insurance purposes. Try to be as thorough as possible. If you must discard some items, then be sure to take pictures and list these items. Use the content damage list available in this book.

Avoid entering any building before local officials have said that it is safe to do so. Buildings may have hidden damage that makes them unsafe. This is especially true of buildings with basements or structures of two or more levels. Gas leaks or electric or waterline damage can create additional problems.

Report broken utility lines to the appropriate authorities. Check with your utility beforehand as to power concerns. In a major catastrophe over a large area it may take the utility company a long time to get to your property. Minimize your risks at all times.

When entering buildings use extreme caution. Building damage may have occurred but be covered by debris. The force of water currents can weaken walls. Examine walls, floors, doors, staircases, and windows to make sure that the building is not in danger of collapsing. Get approval before entering.

Don't smoke, and be alert for fire hazards. Fire is the most frequent hazard following floods. There may be broken or leaking gas lines, flooded electrical circuits, or submerged furnaces or electrical appliances. Flammable or explosive materials may travel from upstream.

Wear sturdy shoes. The most common injury following a disaster is foot injury. This is more dangerous due to sewage and bacteria in water. Make sure that you have had your tetanus shot.

Use battery-powered lanterns or flashlights when examining buildings. Never use open flames or lanterns.

Inspect foundations for cracks or other damage. The swelling of saturated soils or scouring under the foundation can weaken a structure.

Pump out flooded basements gradually (about one-third of the water per day) to avoid structural damage. If the water is pumped completely in a short period of time, pressure from water-saturated soil on the outside could cause basement walls to collapse. Watch for snakes or animals that might have been carried by floodwaters.

Check for gas leaks. If you smell gas or hear a blowing or hissing noise, open a window and quickly leave the building. If you turn off the gas for any reason, it must be turned back on by a professional.

Look for electrical system damage. Be certain to have your home's electrical system checked out by a qualified electrician. This is especially true if your basement was flooded or water reached electrical wiring.

Check for sewage and waterline damage. Flood waters can overwhelm sewage lines causing sewage to back up and flood your home. If water pipes are damaged, then contact the water company and avoid using water from the tap.

Watch for loose ceilings of plaster or drywall that could fall.

Service damaged septic tanks, cesspools, pits, and leaching systems as soon as possible. Damaged sewage systems are health hazards.

The Importance of a "Proof of Loss"

Important: Your official claim for damages requires that you file a "PROOF OF LOSS" This NFIP form must be fully completed and signed and in the hands of your insurance company/adjuster within 60 days after the loss occurs.

In some severe floods FEMA may authorize extensions of time for various form submittals. Check with FEMA, NFIP about extensions of time for submittal, do not presume or take for granted any extension.

The proof of loss includes a detailed estimate to replace or repair the damaged property. The adjuster will often provide you with suggested proof of loss, however you are responsible for making sure that it is complete, accurate and filed in a timely manner. Keep a copy in your own file for your own records.

Refer to your declaration page of your National Flood Insurance Program (NFIP) policy for coverage, limitations, restrictions, and deductibles.

Secure your important papers. You will need these documents and if they are left in a flooded property they can quickly become destroyed.

Five important steps in filing a flood claim:

1 File your claim as quickly as you can. Be certain to get a claim number to assure that you are in the system. Remember, your flood policy is not your normal homeowner's policy. You may be able to file two claims if windblown rain, or roof damage was involved, one with your normal insurance policy and one with your flood insurance policy.

2 Separate your property. Your policy normally requires you to separate damaged property from undamaged property. Don't throw anything away unless local law requires it. Be certain to take detailed photos of any items that are thrown away. When taking pictures take an overview shot of a room and then take the detailed shot of items, including any make or serial numbers

In addition, if you have to remove wall to wall carpet to get to the floor to dry out, then keep a sample of the carpeting and/or flooring to show your adjuster. Document everything.

3 Make a list of damaged contents. Document everything. Use a video camera and take photos of items. Use the content list in this book. You can also ask your adjuster for a sheet to list your damaged contents, but if you wait for the adjuster to respond, then you have waited too long. Begin immediately to list damaged items with a full description. See the chapter in this book on "contents". Remember, it is your job to make this list. You know better than anyone else what "stuff" you have and what you paid for it. Take the time to list it all. This can be tedious work, but it is worth thousands of dollars to you. If you don't complete these lists, you will not receive the reimbursement! Have your whole family get involved by listing the items in each room. Just tell them that if they want to get their stuff back then they had better make their list! If you can salvage receipts, then get them. If you have purchased items on a credit card or check, then you can get old records of purchases from the credit card company or your bank. The NFIP has specific forms for content listing.

4 List areas of structural damage

Use the exterior and interior checklists in this book.

If the water was deep, then there are some things which must be checked by a professional such as an electrician, gas, HVAC, plumber, engineer or a general contractor. If you have any of these professionals visit your home, then be sure to have them give you a written estimate of repair including a written description of what caused the damage and if the item can be repaired or if it must be replaced. Have this information for the adjuster's visit or present it to him/her ASAP. Without this written information, you may not get paid.

5 Your claim is payable after:

a. You and the insurance company agree on the amount of damage. See "Review your Damages, and "Understanding the Adjusters Estimate"

b. The insurer has received your complete accurate and signed "Proof of loss.", along with any other requested forms by The NFIP adjuster

If you have not received enough reimbursement and you will need to supplement your claim, then you will need to complete another proof of loss or supplemental form for the new damages. Review chapter 22 in this book for more information regarding supplementing your claim. Supplementing a flood claim can be extremely difficult and may not always be possible.

Temporary repairs and drying out your property….

You will want the adjuster to get there as soon as possible since you may need to discard items to begin the drying out process. If you need to discard items, try to locate them separately in a garage or shed if possible so that your adjuster can view them. List and photo any items discarded.

Repairs:

If the flooding in your home was minimal, (a few inches) and did not reach your electrical wiring, you may be able to get by with just removing the bottom two feet of drywall or other wall material. Get an electrician to inspect. Remove any wet/damaged building insulation. Treat the area with a mildew/fungicide and dry out as rapidly as possible with dehumidifiers and fans. It is best to have a company that specializes in water extraction to oversee this. However, and this is very important, get an estimate for their work before they do it, you don't want all your insurance money spent in tear out, as their will be far greater expense awaiting ahead in the rebuilding. Get competitive bids and a written description of all work to be done, along with rapid work scheduling. Water damaged materials need to be removed immediately!

Flood waters that come within a property are to be considered as sewage in the drying out and cleanup efforts. The surfaces must be thoroughly sanitized. Surfaces are not merely wet and in need of drying. In some cases, it will be impossible to clean and sanitize.

Take copious pictures before removing any of the contents of your home. (See chapter 15) Contents need to be especially closely examined if they were in any standing water. All wood items in water should be replaced and metal items should be inspected for rust. Metal furniture legs often rust from within, when they have been in standing water. Remember all items must be viewed as having been in sewage.

Most often wood floors will have to come up because of swelling and warping. Tile floors sometimes can be saved. Vinyl and carpet will most often need to be replaced. If these items are removed, be sure to keep a sample of the material for your adjuster to see. Subfloors need to be thoroughly dried.

3c

Fire / Smoke Loss

Of all the different types of property loss, this is probably one of the most devastating. We hope that you have not experienced any loss of life, or injury to your family or pets. The place that most fires begin at home is in the kitchen, not from a faulty appliance, but rather from an unattended dish on the burner.

For success in this claim it is crucial to document the contents of your home. Use the damage checklist to list the destroyed items as soon as possible. Take as many pictures as possible of rooms and possessions. Make sure that smoke damaged items are properly cleaned or replaced. A related issue to a fire loss has to do with water. If the fire company was called and released thousands of gallons of water into your home, then you will have water damage. Remember that water always follows the course of least resistance, so make sure that water damage is thoroughly investigated. It is not within the scope of this chapter to address water damage.

One of the many issues of damage in this type of claim has to do with smoke damage. Smoke travels throughout the home or property as an object is being consumed by flames. Damages may occur not only to structural materials, but also to curtains, clothing, bedding, furniture, rugs and carpeting. The air conditioning system may also become contaminated with soot. It is best to have a professional service that specializes in these types of claims to come to your home and perform an inspection. You will want to have them thoroughly check your rooms and contents and provide you with a written estimate of repair. You should do this ASAP so that you will be able to provide your adjuster with this information. A Public Adjuster can help with all of this.

If the adjuster has already been to your home, then you still need to have a smoke/fire restoration company perform an inspection and estimate so that you can compare it to your adjuster's estimate.

Another issue has to do with the extent of damages. Remember that heat rises and the hot air from a fire will not only damage the area that is being burned, but will also be heaviest directly above that area on the ceilings. A close inspection must be performed to determine if paint has blistered. It is a good idea to have ceiling drywall in the region of the fire removed because it would have been exposed to high heat.

Since most ceilings are made of drywall which has paper and glue as two of its components, it is likely that its structural integrity has been compromised and that it should be replaced. In most cases it is not sufficient to merely paint the damaged area. Attic Insulation and insulation within walls may be contaminated by smoke and should be replaced.

The same is true if there was a fire within a wall cavity. Both sides of the wall will often need to be replaced with further attention being paid to structural studs and beams. If it appears that outlets or electrical wirings were affected, then these items should also be replaced. If the fire in your home was not cooking related, but related to electrical problems, it is necessary that a licensed electrician inspect your home's electrical system. The exterior sheathing of wires can be damage by heat and may need replacement.

During your electrician's inspection, there may come up discussion of ordinance or building code. This will particularly apply to older homes. If you have a covered loss, your policy may have coverage for updates due to building code requirements. Check your policy and speak to your agent. If this coverage is in dispute, then you may need to talk to an attorney.

As previously mentioned, if your heater/air conditioner was on during the fire/smoke then this system should be replaced, or at the least cleaned very thoroughly. Some types of ductwork cannot be adequately cleaned. If the fire occurred in the kitchen do not forget to look underneath the wall cabinets for signs of scorching or discoloration. If the fire occurred on the stove, it will probably be necessary to replace it. This is because the plastic knobs on the stove often melt, along with other plastic components such as clock, timer, etc. If the fire occurred on your stove, it is very likely that your stove vent and ductwork should also be replaced.

Since most insurance policies provide for replacement of like kind and quality, you should insist that all the cabinets in the kitchen be replaced if some of these cabinets were damaged. If, however, your home was newly built and the identical cabinets are still being manufactured, then you may be able to restore your home without replacing all of them. The best thing to do is to have a cabinet company inspect and create a written estimate of repair. If the company does not believe that the cabinetry can be matched perfectly, then have them make a written statement in this regard. Kitchen cabinetry can be many thousands of dollars.

Remember, in most cases your adjuster is not an expert in kitchen cabinetry, heat/air conditioning, electrical, or water damage. Get your own inspection. A Public Adjuster is highly recommended because of the high dollar values, complexities and varieties of damage in a fire/smoke loss.

In a fire, there will be 3 basic types of damages to property and contents and I want to take some time to explain. Some of these are often overlooked.

1) Visible Fire damage from flame and heat:

   It may destroy totally, and turn to ash or vaporize or it may partially burn, scorch or melt. Even items that appear ok, may have heat damage, this especially true with anything plastic.

2) Smoke and soot:

   A fire may appear in the kitchen but smoke and soot can travel through the whole house. Smoke and soot will migrate for many reasons such as:

   Super-heated air in the fire

   Opening in windows and doors, through holes in walls, through plumbing, and electrical openings

   Smoke and soot will travel through the ductwork with the Heat/AC on and even when it is off.

   Fans that may be used to move air through the house in fire extinguishing.

   Fans / Dehumidifiers that will be used to dry out the house

   Carried about by firemen and other cleanup workers

3) Water damage and fungal/mold growth

   When a fire is extinguished with water by the fire company a single truck may discharge 1000 gallons. When hooked up to a fire hydrant a 4-inch fire hose can deliver an average of 500 gallons per minute. Water weighs 8.34 lbs. a gallon, so that's over 4000 lbs. of water in only one minute. This is a lot of water and a tremendous weight burden for the structure to bear.

Water that is sprayed on roof and into attic will migrate through the ceiling, into the walls and down to and through the floor and down into the next level below. A fire in second floor will not only cause water damage on that floor but also in the floor below and even to the basement. Water always seeks its lowest level.

Wet drywall, wood flooring, wooden household items, furniture, fabrics, furnishings, and contents are all subject to the contaminations and must be removed, discarded or properly cleaned.

3d

Hail Loss

The cost of repairing hail in the US averages over 1 Billion per year

It is not unusual for hail damages to be misdiagnosed. Damage is not always consistent and can vary greatly even among homes of proximity. There are numerous factors that can come into play in a hail investigation; this chapter will try to cover many of them.

What causes hail?

In certain circumstances, hot moist air is drawn high into the sky and atmosphere can cause a storm called a supercell. These updrafts carry dirt and dust particles into the high and cold parts of storm clouds. Extremely cold water is attracted to these particles of dust forming very small balls of ice. The combination of falling balls of ice and rising updrafts causes the hail to grow layer upon layer like an onion. Many stones that fall are the size of peas, but on some occasions, they might grow to golf ball or even tennis ball size. On rare occasions hail comes to earth that looks more like crystals.

Challenges of a hail claim.

Often, there is no visible damage on the roof that is observable from the ground. That does not mean, however, that there is not damage. The height of the roof, angle of the roof, ridges, or other obstructions may make the roof unobservable from the ground. It is vital that the roof be inspected from above. Damage from hailstones less than 1.5 inches in size can often be difficult to see. It is important to have a qualified inspector.

Your insurance adjuster must go on the roof to inspect! If, however, an adjuster can determine damages from the roof's edge and determines the roof needs replacement, then it may not be necessary to go on at that time. Just move on with the claim and get it replaced.

If an adjuster looks from the ground, or simply looks from the edge of the roof, and finds "no damage" or wants a "partial repair" then that evaluation must be suspect!

If this is the case, then you MUST have another inspection. This is especially true if many homes in your area are receiving new roofs. You don't have to just accept whatever your insurance adjuster states.

I recommend that a reputable roofer inspect and give you a written report with photos. Be sure to use that roofer for repairs when you get the money since their documentation helped you get it! Please don't take this company's work for granted!

Safety is of the utmost importance! Never go on a roof that is wet from a rainstorm, or icy. Very steep roofs will require special safety equipment.

Some people unwisely have a family member or friend climb up to "take a look" and they often conclude "it looks ok to me". Don't do that! Have a qualified roofer or general contractor skilled at looking at hail damage inspect.

Different types of roofs and construction materials react in different ways. A shingled roof, metal roof or tiled roof will all respond differently to hail strikes. Wood, metal, and vinyl trim also respond differently.

By following the advice below you can determine if a hail investigation is needed and if so, strengthen your insurance claim for repair:

1) The weather report. You can often find this by looking up on line: "Weather report in City / State on Date" or "Hail report in Your (state) on (Date)" Remember, insurance companies also access these reports.

2) If you're at home and heard or saw hail falling, take a video on your phone of hail falling, or pictures of the hailstones. Make sure you can prove that it is at your house by showing your yard, etc. Be certain not to endanger yourself by going into the storm and risk getting hit by hailstones. When safe, pick the hail stones up and measure with a ruler if you can. This is great documentation if you have it! Ask family members or neighbors if they have any video or pictures.

3) If other neighbors are getting new roofs or repairs, speak to them. Ask if their repair was related to hail damage. Write down the door numbers of homes in your community. Inquire at neighbors directly behind, in front of, and beside you. Be a good neighbor and share this information with others.

4) Do your cars, lawn items, deck or fences show dents from hail?

5) Damaged window screens, broken windows, paint chipping on wall finishes, splatter marks or flakes of paint knocked off fences tell a story of hail.

Roof Inspection:

When the roof is being inspected, take note and photographs of damage of:

- Dents on wind turbines

- Dents in metal chimney caps or flashing that cover the chimney flue

- Dents in guttering on the edge or within the basin of guttering

- Dents on valley flashing (that is the thin metal surfaces)

- Dents on drip edge

- Granule loss found in gutters, and base of downspouts on the ground

Hailstone damage can be difficult to determine. Varying factors include:

- Hardness and softness and the size of the hailstone. Some common terms used to describe hailstone size are: pea, marble, dime, penny, nickel, quarter, golf ball, tennis ball, baseball, tea cup, and grapefruit.

- Hail may fall straight down. Hail falling straight down may not do any damage to walls, windows, screens or other trim. Hailstones can be driven sideways by wind. Wind driven hail damage may at times only appear on one side of a building.

- The speed, shape and impact of the hailstone. This speed affects the total weight of impact. For instance, a two-inch hail stone falls around 72 mph a three-inch falls at about 88 mph.

3e

Tornado – Terror from The Sky

Few things in life can be as frightening as a tornado. The sight of a funnel dropping from the clouds even miles away strikes terror in most people's hearts. If your home has been affected or possibly destroyed by a tornado, our hearts go out to you.

There are more tornados in the U.S. annually then in any other nation in the world. Approximately one third of the tornados in the United States occur in a part of the country known as Tornado Alley, comprising the states of Texas, Oklahoma, Kansas, and Nebraska. Most of these tornados occur because of the cold Canadian air and warm gulf air clashing.

If your home has been demolished or moved from its foundation, then it should be totaled and your insurance company should probably pay you your policy limits. You will have to review your policy for this information. More information regarding managing your claim can be found in this book.

Whether your home has been totaled or just partially damaged, don't forget to file a claim for any other structures that you may have or had on your property. Review your policy to see what it says about additional structures, fences, trees, pool enclosures, debris removal, and so forth.

If your home was demolished, you will also want to create a list of your contents. You know better than anyone else what you had in your home. For more detailed information, there is a chapter in this book entitled, contents. For success in this claim it is crucial to document the contents of your home. Use the damage checklists found in this book to list the destroyed or damaged items as soon as possible. Take as many pictures as possible of rooms and possessions.

If your home was not totaled, then you will have to survey the damage closely. Use the damage checklist. This will help your adjuster to estimate the damage, serve as a mirror to check the adjuster's estimate, and be useful for contractors creating an estimate for the repairs.

Oftentimes the severe winds related to a tornado will damage a roof. It is important to try to minimize damage from rain by covering your roof or performing temporary repairs. This book has more information under Duties of Insured after a Loss, in this regard. You should have at least one roofing company come out and inspect your roof and give you a written estimate. If possible, have the roofer go up into the attic area to look for leaks and separation of roof trusses which may have occurred. Roof trusses loosened from the high winds can weaken the structural integrity of your home.

Another place to inspect is windows and doors. Do they rattle or not close and open properly? Use the damage checklist to survey your home closely. If loose roof trusses, doors and windows that won't open or close, new-found cracks in walls, ceiling, or floor, appear, then it is wise to consult with an engineer familiar with structural concerns. In most cases it is well worth the money if he/she finds that your home has been damaged because of the storm. The engineer's report should be in writing and include a detailed plan of repair. A contractor can than write an estimate based upon the engineer's recommendations. Submit both reports to your insurance company.

Remember, in most cases your adjuster is not an expert roofer, engineer, or contractor. Carefully review this information and get the best experts possible. You will be glad that you did!

3f

Earthquake Loss

An earthquake is a sudden and rapid shaking of the earth caused by the breaking and shifting of rock beneath the earth's surface. This shaking can sometimes trigger landslides, avalanches, flash floods, fires and tsunamis.

The worst earthquake in recent history resulting in 280,000 deaths occurred on December 26, 2004. This was a magnitude 9.0 earthquake, about 100 miles west of Sumatra, 6.2 miles under the Indian Ocean. This earthquake triggered a series of tsunamis that sent waves of water crashing into at least half a dozen countries across Southern Asia.

In the United States about 5,000 quakes can be felt each year. Since 1900, earthquakes have occurred in 39 states and caused damage in all 50. One of the most famous faults along which earthquakes are sometimes felt is the San Andreas Fault, which extends about 600 miles through California.

Earthquakes in the United States are not covered under standard homeowners' or business insurance policies. Coverage is usually available for earthquake damage in the form of an endorsement.

Earthquake insurance provides coverage for the shaking and cracking that may destroy buildings and personal possessions.

Coverage for other kinds of damage that may result from earthquakes, such as fire and water damage due to burst gas and water pipes, is provided by standard home and business insurance policies.

Earthquake insurance carries a deductible, usually in the form of a percentage of the replacement cost limit rather than a dollar amount. This deductible varies. In most cases, property owners can get higher deductibles to save money on earthquake premiums. You will need to review your policy.

Immediately after an earthquake you should....

Inspect the entire length of chimneys carefully for damage. Be alert when near chimneys. Since chimneys are freestanding masonry they are especially susceptible to cracking. They should be checked out by a professional to avoid a fire during later usage.

Stay out of damaged buildings. If you are away from home, return only when authorities say that it is safe. Aftershocks can cause further damage. If you need to get back into your home, have someone remain outside to observe and call for help if necessary.

Watch animals closely. Some animals can become agitated during and after an earthquake.

When entering buildings, use extreme caution. Building damage may have occurred yet not be readily visible. Roof trusses or wall supports may have come loose.

Check for gas leaks. Fire is one of the most common dangers after an earthquake. If you smell gas or hear hissing or a blowing noise leave the building quickly. Turn off the gas at the outside main valve and call the gas company from a neighbor's home. Your gas must be turned back on by a professional.

Check your water heater, gas heater, gas stove or other gas appliances. Sometimes couplings can come loose. Consider strapping these items to the wall to prevent future movement. If you don't have flexible fittings, then consider having these installed.

Look for electrical system damage. If you see sparks, broken or frayed wires, or if you smell something burning, turn off the electricity at the main fuse box or circuit breaker. Don't step in water when near electrical systems. Call a licensed electrician for inspection. Have him give you a written description of damages and their causation along with an estimate for repair.

Check for sewage and water line damage. If you suspect sewage or water pipes are damaged, contact the water company and avoid using water from the tap.

Look in cabinets or on floors for any chemicals such as cleaners, paints, bleach, etc. that may have fallen off shelves and broken open. Some may have toxic odors, so be cautious.

If your home is safe, then....

Take pictures of the damage. Begin on the outside and work your way around the inside. Use the exterior and interior damage checklists available in this book. You will want to give a copy of this list to your adjuster and to your contractor. Take special note above doorways, above and below windows, and wall and ceiling corners.

If possible if your home is safe, go into, or have someone go into your attic to inspect your roof trusses. Make sure that they are firmly attached at the center ridge and to the walls. If you see daylight or suspect leaks, then call a roofer.

If your home has a basement and it is safe, go into it and look for any cracks in wall materials. Be alerted to note damage and take photos and note which wall is cracked. Not only may your structure's integrity be compromised, but you might find water leaking in during the next heavy rain so, pay careful attention, especially in corners of walls, floor and ceiling.

Walk around the outside of your house and look for cracks in wall corners, along mortar lines, and on the foundation. Pay attention above and below windows and doors. Check to see if your house is bolted to its foundation. Homes that are not bolted have been known to move or slide off of their foundations, sometimes bringing destruction. If your home is bolted, inspect these bolts and if it not bolted, then consider having this done.

If you believe that the foundation has been affected, have it inspected by a foundation company and/or an engineer. Have these professionals give you a written report as to the extent and cause of damage. Have a written estimate of repair and give a copy of this to your adjuster when he arrives.

If your home has a deck or porch see if it seems loose or if nails or tie-ins have broken free. Look at the floor supports and at the trellis or roof line. Remember you may have coverage for other structures. Review chapter on coverage and as always, check your policy.

If your home has a pool take note of the water level and check it again each day for a week or so. It may be leaking water. This water, if allowed to leak, may damage your home's foundation or that of your neighbor, so be alert.

Consider having your building evaluated by a professional engineer that specializes in building inspections. Have the engineer give you a written evaluation of damage and a repair plan. This is especially important if there seems to be more extensive damage than merely superficial minor cracks. Be sure to examine other areas such as porches, front and back decks, sliding glass doors, canopies, carports, and garage doors. Be careful to follow local building codes regarding construction as they are designed for your safety.

4

Your Insurance Claim: A Call to Action!

The filing of an insurance claim is a call to action on your part and a call to action on the part of your insurance company. Begin by following these four proven steps to ensure that you recover enough to restore your home and get the money you deserve!

Call to action #1 Inspect your home or property!

No one knows your home or business as well as you do! You have probably lived or worked there for years. It is up to you to go outside and give your home a good looking over. If you weren't at home when the catastrophe hit how will you know if there is damage? Perhaps you were inside seeking shelter. The only way to know the scope of damage is to walk the perimeter of your property. You must look meticulously, you must look thoroughly and you must take notes.

You must pay attention to detail. Look at your fence, your yard, your storage shed or garage. Look at your roof (any misplaced shingles), your rain gutters, your shutters, windows, doors, etc. Then you need to go inside and with your damage checklist note all damages listing every room and every surface. The damage checklist found in this book is the quick and easy way to do this.

Call to action #2 Review your policy!

Get your property owners policy and read it over carefully. The first page is normally your declaration page. It usually contains "the six p's" which are: Property owner, Property address, Perils insured, Policy Limits, Period of Coverage, Premium Paid. The first thing you must do is make sure that your damage is listed under your covered perils. The rest of your policy will help define this information. If you get stuck or can't find your policy, then call your insurance agent. He/she will be able to provide you with a copy and answer questions.

If your loss is a covered loss, then you need to look at your deductible. The deductible is the amount of money that you must pay before your insurance company will pay. Look carefully at the amount of your deductible. You may have several different types of deductibles. If you live along a coastal state prone to hurricanes, then you might have a separate windstorm policy, so be sure to check this deductible also.

Call to Action #3 Compare your damages to your deductible!

This is the magic equation. If you have completed a damage checklist this one is a piece of cake! If you haven't done #1 thoroughly yet, or don't know exactly what to look for, then use the "Damage Checklist" found in chapter 16. It will help you detail everything room by room. If you don't have any idea what it will cost to fix all the things you see wrong, then a good idea is to call a general contractor. Ask if you can read him your list to determine if it is above your deductible or not. The contractor will give you an idea if your claim is above the deductible. Do you see how important steps #1, and #2 is? If your damages then exceed your deductible, then you should file your claim.

Call to action #4 File your claim!

This fourth and final call to action on your part requires a call to action on the part of the insurance company. Many people file their claim by calling their agent, or by calling a toll-free number for claims. When you call, provide your name as stated on your policy, your policy number, and your home, work and cell phone number. Make sure that you receive a claim number. Until you have a claim number, don't presume that your claim is opened.

5

Documentation

If you could only read one chapter in this book, then read this one.

You'd be foolish to stop here however.

Do these steps and you will be way ahead of most!

It is crucial in the handling of your claim that careful records be kept.

This system need not be complicated, but it must be present...

I suggest that you put together all the following:

1) Get a large manila folder, or better yet an expandable file in which you can place all the items related to your claim. This is crucial!

This folder will have all claim items. Put it in a place that is readily available and where you can get to it quickly if you receive a call from your insurance company. After all, you will want to take notes!

2) After you have read this book from cover to cover, place it in your file for further reference.

3) A yellow note pad so that you can take claim related notes and have a permanent record. All in one place!

4) Your declaration page. (to be explained later)

5) Your insurance policy.

6) Your own photos of your damaged property.

7) Photos of damaged contents.

8) Your personal set of "damage checklists". (to be explained later)

9) All letters and email correspondence from your insurance company.

10) All letters and emails from you to your insurance company.

11) Estimates that you might obtain.

12) An envelope to insert receipts from any expenses that you may incur.

Please trust me on the importance of this. I believe that most claims can be settled without legal intervention. However, good record keeping is important. Your claim is too important to rely upon memory or "He said, she said". DOCUMENTATION IS CRUCIAL.

No one cares about your claim as much as you do! No one knows as much about your claim as you do! You can be certain that the insurance company is keeping a file on your claim. Shouldn't you do the same? You need to protect your investment! Also, accidents can happen to insurance company files and documents can occasionally become lost or displaced. I have experienced that before. So, it is crucial that you have an accurate record of your claim. If you later seek the service of a public adjuster or an attorney, they will ask for your records to date on your claim. These professionals will need this so that he/she can accurately surmise your case. Your records are valuable. Don't presume that the insurance company will have them all and that you can get them later from them.

In summary: Watch out for your interests and peace of mind by keeping careful documentation together in a file.

6

Correspondence

Although this chapter is primarily common sense, it is very important for the success of your claim.

Here is an outline of how all your correspondence to the insurance company should look. It needs to have the following information. The purpose of each letter will vary and will be reflected in the body text of the letter. Separate body texts of letters will be given for various situations throughout this book. Whenever sending something in correspondence to your insurance company it is wise to send it certified, return receipt requested. That way you will know exactly when it was received and who signed for it. Oftentimes family members may be handling your file. You do not want things to get lost. You also want to keep an exact copy of your correspondence in your file. If you have noticed that there seems to be a pattern of lack of follow-through or responsiveness, then you will especially want to send this letter certified, return receipt. A fax might be acceptable if you print and keep a record of the transmission. Emails have become very popular and are now commonplace. Be certain to request a read receipt. If you feel you are being ignored or are not receiving proper response to emails or phone calls, a certified letter with return receipt, is excellent. In that it enables you to see who signed for the document, along with a date of reception. At the risk of seeming elementary I present the following as a suggested format in your correspondence:

Your name (Exactly as it appears on your policy)

Your Mailing Address

City, State, Zip code

Area code, Phone Number

Date of letter

To: Adjuster or department name

Insurance Company: Insurance Company Name

Adjuster Street Address   Number, Address, Suite #

P.O. Box   if any

City, State, Zip   City, State, Zip

Reference:

Property Address: Your properties Street # Unit #, City, State, ZIP

Policy Number: Your Policy number

Claim Number: Your Claim number

Date of Loss: Date damage occurred

Dear (adjuster name / claims dept.)

Body Text. (This is where you will include confirmation of correspondence, discussion, phone calls, raise concerns and or present information.)

I look forward to a prompt response.

Sincerely,

Your Signature
Your name typed

7

Handling Phone Calls

Phone calls are an important part of resolving your claim.

There is an old saying "the squeaky wheel gets the grease". This is true! Sometimes a series of phone calls can be very effective in moving your claim forward.

You should always have a note pad or paper on hand when dealing with your insurance company. You will want to write down the name of the person you spoke with, the time, and the date.

If you left a voice mail write down the contents of your message.

If you spoke to a person who took a message, ask for that person's name and the name of who will be calling back.

Always ask "when should I expect to hear back?" and then wright that down.

Every phone call should be for moving your claim forward. Be certain that you have asked for whatever the next step will be.

Whenever you make or receive a phone call be certain to have your legal notepad from your file at hand.

If you are initiating the call, then be certain you have written down your questions beforehand. You want to know what kind of answers you are looking for. When you ask your questions to the adjuster write down his/her responses under the questions that you have already written out.

If the adjuster makes statements or questions you then need to write down his questions and your responses. It is very crucial that you write down this conversation. Don't rely on your memory, and don't forget that the adjuster has many claims going on that might be like yours.

If there are any statements made as to what the insurance company is going to do, then always ask for a time frame. If the adjuster says, "in the next few days" then write that down. If they say, "next week" write it down, and ask "when next week?" If the adjuster does not give a time frame, then ask for a specific day and possibly time.

If the adjuster says that "certain steps must occur", then ask the adjuster "what those steps are and who will be involved". Write all this information down.

Whenever you have a phone conversation with the insurance adjuster, it is a very good idea to send a letter of confirmation of the phone call. This can also be done by email. This is especially true if the adjuster has committed to accomplishing certain tasks or if he was expecting you to follow through on anything.

If you have noticed that there seems to be a pattern of lack of follow-through or responsiveness then you may want to send this letter certified, return receipt. Emails are also acceptable but be sure to request a read receipt so you know that it has been viewed and when it was viewed.

A good practice whenever emailing your adjuster is to request an email response confirming his/her reception and ability to open any attachments.

The following is a sample format of a follow up letter or email to a phone call:

Your name (Exactly as it appears on your policy)

Your policy #

Claim #

Your Mailing Address

City, State, Zip code

Area code, Phone Number

Date of letter

To: Adjuster or department name

Insurance Company: Insurance Company Name

Adjuster Street Address Number, Address, Suite #

P.O. Box   if any

City, State, Zip   City, State, Zip

Dear (Adjuster name)

I am writing to confirm our phone discussion of day/month/year.

As you will recall, "I called You / You called me…" During that call we discussed "_____" You asked me "_____" and I replied "_____" You told me that "_____" I asked you "_____" and you replied to me that "_____" You also said that you were going to do "_____".

You asked me for the "_____" I am gathering that information and will send it …

I asked you "_____"and you responded "_____"

In our conversation, you told me that I could expect to hear from you by "_____
Date_____"

I await your response,

Sincerely

Your Signature
Your name typed

8

Understanding Your Policy - Your Contract with Your Insurance Company

The only way to be sure of what your policy states is by reading it yourself. If you are still confused you may need to talk to your agent. If that does not satisfy, you may want to seek legal counsel. Even then, it may be unclear as to what the interpretation of the policy is. An astute, experienced, up-to-date lawyer in this field of law is your best source of information.

This book does not seek to give legal advice nor should it be assumed as such. Your policy is your legal contract. Questions regarding your contract should be directed to your agent or attorney.

The information in this chapter is given in terms of generalities not specifics. Your policy may define something differently and your state may interpret the terms of your contract differently. Consult a lawyer if you have questions with your policy. I am not a lawyer.

With that being said…

Your Declaration Page- What is it?

Your declaration page "declares" the specific items that are exclusive to your policy with the insurance company. It is composed most often of six primary sections. These may be called the "Six P's" and are a summary of your particular policy. Take your declaration page in hand and locate the following items:

Persons Insured

Policy Number

Property Location

Perils Insured Against

Period or Term of Coverage

Premium Paid

Here is an explanation of each of these items:

Person Insured:

This section names the insured and gives the mailing address. The persons insured section may also have the name of your Mortgage Company or bank if there is an insured interest in your property. When the time comes for the insurance company to issue payment for your damage, in most cases the names of these parties will be on the check. The exception to this is typically regarding contents (furniture, household good, etc.) and loss of use coverage (if you need to move out of your home and incur expense)

Policy Number:

This number is unique and is assigned only to your individual policy. It may have both letters and numbers. This is the number that your agent and insurance company use in referencing your policy. This number should be included on all correspondence between you and your insurance company.

Property Location:

This gives the physical address of the property which is insured. If your home or property needs to be visited by your adjuster this is the address that they will go to.

Perils Insured Against:

This is an overview of the coverage for which you have contracted with the insurance company. A peril is the cause of a loss. Your policy may cover such perils as hurricane, flood, hail, windstorm, fire, etc. It is important to be aware of what perils you are insured for, and the limit of liability (maximum amount payable to you or others if a covered loss occurs). The three most common forms of coverage are dwelling, personal property, and liability. There may be other coverage such as loss of use, loss assessment, there is a wide variety of forms of coverage, including loss of use and loss assessment.

Period or Term of Coverage:

This is the coverage period. It begins on a certain date and concludes on a later date, normally a one-year period. It is important to note that if you file a claim with your insurance company, then the claim will have a date of loss. This date of loss may or may not be the day you filed your claim. The date of loss will be the day that your actual loss was sustained or discovered in most cases. The policy that was in effect on this date of loss will be the one that your claim will be filed under. Be sure to look at the policy period to be sure that you are reading the policy that is in effect at the time of loss. Policies can and do change with time and at renewals.

Premium Paid:

This is the amount of money that you will pay for the insurance company to provide the coverage which is stated for the prescribed period.

9

Your Deductible

In many cases this is a percentage of the overall policy limits of your claim. On properties of the same value, typically the higher your deductible the lower your premium will be. The deductible for a million-dollar home will be different than that of a one hundred-thousand-dollar home. In some states, there may be a separate deductible for hurricane, windstorm, flood, earthquake or some other catastrophic event. This deductible may be higher. This is particularly true for states which have coastal areas susceptible to hurricanes.

It is important to read your entire policy or policies, because there may be other deductibles or limits of liability that are not found on your declaration page. For instance, you might have a separate deductible or limit on tree removal, debris removal, or fences or enclosed patio covers. You need to read your policy carefully because policies can, and do, differ from one another. If you are unsure what your policy states, then speak to your agent. He/she should be able to help you.

Other items of your policy include:

Loss of Use coverage:

This is the amount of coverage available to you if your home becomes uninhabitable. If you must evacuate, or your home is damaged and it is not safe to live in, or if it will be necessary to move out while certain repairs are made, then this coverage should pay for these additional expenses. (More on this subject will be presented later under "Loss of Use".

Endorsements:

This is additional coverage that you pay for. This might include special coverage for jewelry, rare goods, art, etc. Or, if you live in a community with agreements and covenants, it is possible that your community might call for a special property owner assessment due to damages. If that is a possibility, you should have this additional coverage.

The Agent Who Sold the Policy:

This is the agent's name, address, and phone number who sold you the policy.

Your agent might be the first one to call if you need to file a claim. He/she can provide you with the phone number to file a claim or they might assist you in filing your claim. If you email your claim notification or information you should copy your agent, so he/she is aware. He or she can also make available to you a copy of your declaration page and policy if it has been lost or destroyed.

10

Your Coverage

Many coverage terms are commonplace however you must read your policy. Do not presume anything. It must be in writing in your policy.

It is important to note that other information may also be present on your declaration page. Review your declaration page carefully. Although they are similar in content, every declaration page varies.

Your policy has several components that are commonplace.

Dwelling coverage

This will be a description of the perils that are covered.

Most policies include: fire and lightning, smoke, windstorm, hail, explosion, aircraft and vehicles, vandalism, riot and civil commotion, falling objects, theft. Your policy may also include accidental discharge and sinkhole coverage. Please note that this is not a guaranteed list. You must read your own policy. It is your own policy that covers or excludes perils.

Personal property

This is coverage for physical loss to the property damaged by one of the named perils which are insured in the dwelling section of the policy. Personal property includes things such as household goods, furniture, bedding, clothing, etc. There may be some items that are excluded. Be certain to read your policy.

Liability coverage

Under this category is the limits of personal liability and medical coverage

Personal liability

Personal liability coverage is to protect the insured if a claim is made or a suit is brought against you for damages because of bodily injury or property damage caused by an occurrence to which the coverage applies. Read you policy for more details. This book does not seek to address this issue in depth. Please speak with your agent or an attorney if you need clarification.

Medical payments to others

This coverage is to pay for the medical expenses of someone injured on your property's location. It may also include injury to another that is caused by your activities or that of an animal owned by you. There are limitations to this coverage. Again, please be certain to read your policy. This book does not seek to address this issue in depth. Please speak with your agent or an attorney if you need clarification.

Exclusions

This is a list of items or situations which may be excluded from coverage. Only a review of your specific policy can determine exactly what these exclusions are. Some common exclusions may be cloth awnings, greenhouses, loss by rats, termites, moths or insects, rot, rust, wear or deterioration and smoke from agricultural or industrial operations.

Although many of these items are excluded, it should be noted that if damage occurs by a covered loss, then it might not be excluded. For instance, although rust is normally excluded, if a roof is damaged in a windstorm and water comes in and then an item in the house rusts, then the damage to that item would probably be covered.

Another issue might be mold. There may be some coverage in your policy regarding mold remediation, or it may be excluded, or it might not be mentioned at all. However, if mold growth appears because of a covered loss, then there may be coverage since it might be consequential or indirect loss. Some policies exclude mold/fungi, while others may have limited amount of coverage, careful review is necessary

Coverage questions can sometimes be complex and often may need to be interpreted by legal counsel. Read your policy carefully regarding exclusions. You may actually have coverage if the damage was from an ensuing loss caused by an insured peril. It is not within the scope of this book to provide legal counsel.

If your business operates out of home or you have a commercial policy for your property there will undoubtedly be many additional aspects of your coverage. ALWAYS read your policy over thoroughly, clarify questions with your agent, and or adjuster. A public adjuster is usually very familiar with different types of coverages. An attorney knowledgeable in property and casualty can review your policy and answer legal questions.

11

How to File Your Claim

If you have discovered damage to your home that you feel necessitates your filing a claim with your insurance company, then the following information will be helpful.

The first thing that you should do is to make sure your family is safe. If your home is a hazard or un-inhabitable, then you may need to move out until repairs are made. Many insurance policies have some sort of "loss of use" coverage, but it is best to talk with your insurance company before supposing that you are qualified to receive this coverage. You will also need to know the financial limitations of your policy which is unique in this regard, you must review it.

Temporary Repairs should be made if the damage is exposing the interior to the elements. If your roof is leaking, at least try to have a tarp attached or patch made. If windows are blown out or a wall damaged then try to board them up to prevent further intrusion of flood or rainwater, wind and the elements. This can prevent further damage and help prevent theft, insect or pest invasion. You will need to closely examine your home.

Timing is crucial. It is best to file your claim immediately at the time of loss. Do not hesitate or forget to file your claim. If you fail to file a claim your insurance company may have the right to later deny your claim if too much time has elapsed. The limitations of this period will usually be defined in your policy.

Occasionally a property may experience damage but the owner does not recognize that there is damage until a time, weeks or even months later. If this is the case, then file your claim at the time of discovery. Review your policy and then file your claim. So, take the time to be thorough now! It can save future claim problems and damage to your home.

The most common way of filing a claim is to phone it in. Many property owners begin the filing of their claim by calling their agent. Typically, the insurance agent will then assist them. Your agent may give you a phone number to call.

Occasionally an agent may call your claim in for you. During the phone call, the insurance company representative will then take your name, phone number and policy number and ask for a brief description of the damage. At that time, the insurance representative will either give you a claim number or will call you back with a claim number. If your insurance company does not give you a claim number or call back within a day or two with a number, then don't assume that your claim has been filed.

A True Story

I once had a claim in Florida. The homeowners were a couple in their seventies, who lived in a condo along the coast. Due to hurricane damage, they called in a claim to their insurance company. Someone on the phone took their information and told them that they would have someone call once a claim number had been assigned. After a week, no one had called back, so they called again, only to be told the same. The property owners then forgot about their claim, reasoning that the insurance company would eventually get to them. They knew insurance companies were busy from the hurricane. Indeed, over 180 units in their own 200+ condominium complex had damage. When I first met this couple five months after the storm, no contact had been initiated by the insurance company. When we began the process of assisting them with their claim, we found that there was no record of the claim on the insurance company's files. When we reported the claim again we had to provide documentation that the homeowner had already reported the claim. Fortunately, the homeowners had a few notes that they had taken of their own, and we were able to finally open the claim.

Moral of the story: Although this story is an exception to the rule, and most insurance companies are efficient, always make sure that you receive a claim number as soon as possible. This can help assure you that your claim is in the system and enables you and your insurance company to make quick reference to the status of your claim. (Note: On some occasions, your claim number might be the same as that of your policy).

It is very important to write down the claim number and the name and phone number of the adjuster if it has been provided. Usually within a day or two an adjuster will be assigned to your claim. Once an adjuster is assigned a visit will be scheduled.

In a catastrophic situation where many properties in each local are affected (like a hurricane, earthquake, hail storm, tornado) it may take several days or possible weeks before an adjuster actually visits your property. If an adjuster has not scheduled a visit within the first ten to fifteen days after filing your claim, you should contact your insurance company. Give them your claim number and name. By that time, they should be able to give you the name and phone # of the adjuster who has been assigned to your claim. You may need to call him her directly to schedule a visit.

The superior way to file your claim is by certified, return receipt mail. Another way is to file by email but be certain to request a response and a read receipt. With this you will know exactly when your claim file was received and by whom. Even if you filed your claim by phone, it is still a good thing to have a paper record. All correspondence with your insurance company should have: Your name (as it appears on your policy), your mailing address, your property address, your policy #, your date of loss.

It should be addressed to your insurance company (ask your agent if you are unsure of the address). Here is a sample:

Your Name (As it appears on your policy)

Address

Phone

Policy Number

Claim #

Insurance Company

Insurance Address

Date

Dear Claims Department:

I/we are writing to inform you that our property at the above address has been damaged as a result of the recent _____ (event). This event occurred on M/D/Y Could you please send someone to inspect my/our home? I/we can best be reached at home ( ) ___-____- or work/cell ( ) ___-____.

Your prompt attention to this matter is appreciated.

Sincerely,

Your Signature

Your name typed

Email address

Phone #

The next important step you will want to do is to begin to build a file of all the pertinent information review the chapter 5 on "Documentation".

Although you may file your claim by phone it is important to follow up the filing of your claim with a letter and /or email. You should copy your agent regarding this correspondence.

Remember, it is important that you have in writing a record of all correspondence, communications, and conversations. So, confirm the opening of your claim and expectation of an adjusters visit. It should be addressed to your insurance company and my read something like this

Your Name (As it appears on your policy)

Address

Phone

Policy Number

Claim #

Insurance Company

Insurance Address

Date

Dear (Claim Dept./ Adjuster)

This letter serves as confirmation to my phone conversation of month/day/ year with Name_____ Of Department Name, I have been assigned a claim number of #_____ I await an adjuster's visit to my property.

Thank you for your help.

Sincerely,

Your Signature

Your name typed

Email:

Phone:

12

Your Duties after a Loss

Before we begin discussing what to do at the time of loss, we need to define what a loss is. Although upon reading your policy you might think that a certain type of damage is not covered, it is wise to take note of the different types of losses. If you have specific coverage questions you should consult with your agent and possibly with an attorney especially if there is doubt or confusion.

A loss can be defined as an unintentional decline, removal or disappearance of value. There are basically three different categories of a loss. These types are Direct, Indirect or Consequential.

A direct loss is the result of a covered peril. The occurrence of a direct loss immediately diminishes value of the insured property

An indirect loss, is not a direct loss from a covered peril, but the result of one. An indirect loss may cause greater financial damage than a direct loss. For instance, a store may have a fire that caused $1,000 dollars in direct damage. However, since the store was closed for ten days, it may have an indirect loss of $10,000 dollars because of the lost sales and revenue it would have had if it was opened.

A consequential loss is the result of a direct loss and is normally associated with a change in value or condition because of a direct loss.

Your duties after loss are stated clearly in your insurance policy. You need to read and understand these.

The duties may include:

Give prompt written notice of the facts regarding the claim. Although many claims are initiated by a phone call to the insurance company, it is always good to have a written record of the filing of your claim. Put it in writing and send it certified return receipt so that you can be certain that the notification of your claim was received. If emailed always request a read receipt.

Notify the police in the case of theft. This is self-explanatory if a crime has been committed, then report it.

Protect your property from further damage. If you merely walk away from your damaged property, and damages grow worse, then it can be argued that you did not live up to your contractual obligations to protect the property. If your property is damaged and you do not seek to repair or mitigate your damages, you may have difficulty settling your claim and you might even be denied some or all your coverage.

If your home or property has been damaged and you need to perform sudden or temporary repairs, then try to photograph these damages. For instance, if you have fallen trees on your property, or roof, and if your roof is missing shingles or has a hole in it, then photograph it before implementing a temporary fix. If you have a leaking plumbing fixture or appliance and there is water on your carpets or floorings, then take a picture of it before you attempt to dry it out. Remember, in a catastrophic situation, it may be several weeks or even before an adjuster can be there to see the damage. Pictures are crucial to the successful resolution of your claim.

If your home is damaged, for example, windows are broken in a hurricane or tornado or your roof is damaged, you are responsible to make reasonable and necessary repairs to protect your property. This is done to prevent further intrusion of the elements into your home which could create even more damage. It is important to keep any receipts for items purchased or services rendered by people for these repairs. Not only may you be reimbursed from your insurance company for these expenses, but these receipts serve as proof of your sincere attempt to protect your property and minimize the damages.

Furnish an inventory of damaged personal property

This list should show the quantity, description and amount of loss. (for more information see the chapter 15 on contents). Be certain to provide a completed checklist of damaged contents. Remember to take pictures of damaged property before it is discarded. If possible keep it until an adjuster can view it for his/her self. If items are damaged and they still have value, then the insurance company has a right to it as salvage, if they pay you the replacement value.

As often as is reasonably required you should:

Provide the insurance company with access to your damaged property

Provide pertinent records, or documents as requested and permit the making of copies

Submit to examination under oath. If this is requested, then you should consider obtaining legal counsel first.

If requested, provide a signed sworn proof of loss:

A proof of loss, which is a signed statement affirming your damages should be accompanied by an estimate for repair and documentation.

13

Duties of Your Insurance Company after a Loss

Within a short period - usually 15 days (the period should be specified in your policy) after the insurance company receives written notice of your claim they should:

1) Acknowledge receipt of your claim

2) Begin any investigation of the claim

3) Specify any information that they need in relation to your loss or your performance of your duties after loss.

After this, in most cases, the insurance company must notify you in writing regarding the status of your claim as to whether the claim is going to be paid or denied. If there is need for further investigation, then they should put that in writing.

Reservation of Rights

Sometimes after acknowledging your claim in writing, the insurance company may issue you a letter which contains the phrase "reservation of rights".

A reservation of rights letter means that although the insurance company may be investigating your claim, they "reserve the right "to deny or not pay all or part of your claim. The act of investigation usually does not automatically mean that the loss is a covered loss. If you receive this letter be sure to keep it in your correspondence file. If you do not receive a letter such as this, then take note of that also.

In some states failure to send a "reservation of rights" letter may mean that the insurance company may have estopped or given up their right to deny coverage. If you feel that this is the case with your claim, you may want to seek legal counsel or the assistance of a public adjuster.

14

Receipts and Expenses

It is very important to keep a collection of receipts that you may incur.

The expenses fall into several categories. You will want to have an envelope in which to place the receipts for any of these items.

If you don't have an invoice, then look for a cancelled check. If you are paying by cash, then obtain a receipt for goods or services from the person that you hired to do the work. All receipts should give the date, worker or company's name, phone #, address, the work performed and the amount paid.

Even if the amount seems small, it is important to keep the receipt because it serves as testimony that you have tried to minimize the damages by affecting some sort of repair.

Your policy will provide further definition of customary expenses.

a) Loss of Use

If your home has become uninhabitable because of the loss and you need to seek other lodging, then these expenses may be covered. If you have this coverage, then your policy should specify the limits of such.

You should keep a record of:

All hotel, or motel charges

Meal charges

Extra gasoline expenses

Pet kennel charges

Extra phone expenses

Extra utility expenses

Extra clothing/replacement expenses

Laundry or dry-cleaning expenses

Extra phone expenses

Extra expenses if incurred to re-establish a home office.

If possible, it is good to speak with the adjuster before incurring these expenses. If you had to begin incurring these expenses before an adjuster contacted you, then notify the adjuster as quickly as possible.

Another time that loss of use coverage may be available is during repair time.

b) Temporary Repairs and Repairs to Mitigate Damages

Expenses for immediate repair

Whenever possible you should have the adjuster participate in approving these expenses, however if the adjuster has not yet arrived and the delay of repairing the property will cause further damage, then it is usually wise to have these repairs done.

Always try to take photos of any damaged areas, especially if the repairs are going to be performed before the adjuster arrives.

It is important that if a temporary repair is performed that you save the receipt from the individual or company performing the repair. If the person or company performing a temporary repair is likely to be the one performing a complete repair or re-installing a replacement item, then have them give you a written estimate for repair on a separate document. This estimate should be for the replacement of the item(s) in like kind and quality if possible.

Important time and money saving advice:

If you have a tradesman, such as an air conditioner repairman, plumber, electrician, roofer, etc. visit your damaged property have them do the following:

1) Have tradesman or professionals write down specifically what is wrong with any item that they inspect. Make sure they mention, manufacturer and model number if available. Be specific and state what caused the damage

2) If they know the cause of damage, then have them write that down also.

3) If an item will require replacement then have the tradesman write down why it needs to be replaced and why a simple repair is not sufficient.

4) If an item can have a temporary repair, specify the cost then specify what the permanent repair cost will be in writing.

5) If an item can be repaired but will not be warrantable, then have this specified in writing. If the item has been under warranty but is damaged due to a loss covered by your insurance company. Then the item should be replaced with a warrantable replacement.

6) If an item needs to be replaced then have the tradesman give you an estimate for replacement on a separate letterhead. (You may want to obtain another estimate for repair)

A True Story

I was helping a property owner on the Atlantic coast of Florida with a Hurricane loss. There was extensive roof damage and there was water damage to some of the interior ceilings, walls and floor coverings. After the storm, the property owners noticed the AC system was not acting properly.

They called an AC repairman who came to their home and said that the unit needed to be replaced. He gave them written estimate more than five thousand dollars to replace the unit. We filed this information with the claim when we met with the adjuster. The adjuster took this into consideration, but later told us that the estimate to replace the air conditioning unit was not sufficient detailed enough to approve paying the claim.

The insurance company wanted a diagnosis as to what had caused the damage and why it was necessary to replace the whole unit. (After all, maybe the unit was just old, or was not properly maintained...) This required that the homeowner contact the air conditioning company again and request additional documentation in regard to the necessity of replacement. This whole process slowed down the payment of the claim by several weeks.

Moral of the story: Save time, money and possible denials by having your repair person provide a thorough written analysis as to what caused the damage and why replacement is necessary, rather than mere repair. You don't want to have to pay him for a second visit and you don't want to experience more delays with the settlement of your claim.

Temporary repairs may include:

    Temporary Roof Repairs

    Plumbing repairs

    Electrical Repairs

    Air Conditioning repairs

    Heater repairs

    Water extraction services employed to dry floors, carpeting etc.

    Carpet removal

    Drywall removal

    Window repair

    Exterior structural repairs

If the property owner or the insured is the one performing any of these repairs, then be certain to keep all receipts for any materials and photograph your repairs. These serve to document your attempts to prevent further damage to the property.

c) Expense for Debris Removal

Again, it is very important to photograph damages to these items. If debris must be disposed of, then create an itemized list. Whenever possible, do not discard damaged household items until an adjuster has seen and recorded the items.

Here is a list of a few possible items for removal. In most cases your policy will probably provide coverage.

Tree removal

Brush removal

Fence removal

Debris blown in by winds

Debris brought in by flood waters

Damaged or destroyed goods within the household

Carpet, rugs, hardwood floors

Always seek to keep household items until after the adjuster has documented the damage. Begin to document these items as soon as you can and present this list to your adjuster.

15

Your Property's Contents

First, it, is important to try to document all items that are damaged. First prize goes for a photo of the damaged item with a list detailing the item(s). If you can preserve the items until the adjuster arrives, then do so.

Personal Property limits are listed on your "Declaration Page" of your policy.

This is an important issue and I have seen many claims for structural damage in which the damage to contents was overlooked or severely underestimated. Protect your interests! Be sure to create a detailed list with photographs of every damaged item in your home or property. You will want this to be part of documentation you give your adjuster.

In your policy, you will find more information regarding personal property limitations, values and possible exclusions. You will also be able to determine if you have replacement cost (R.C.) coverage or actual cash value (ACV) coverage. Although your policy may cover replacement cost, your insurance company will most likely consider the age of your item and deduct an amount for depreciation. They will then pay you what they call the actual cash value. If you choose to replace the item and purchase a like item, then you must submit a receipt of this purchase to your insurance company. They should reimburse you the depreciation for that item if it is equal to the amount of depreciation withheld. To get full payment for your contents, some insurance companies may want you to furnish them with a receipt for replacement before paying fully.

Important: If recoverable depreciation has been withheld, don't expect your insurance company to chase you down for receipts. When they issue you a check for your contents there will usually be a letter accompanying it in which you will find reference to recovery of this depreciation. It is likely that this will be the last letter you will see in this regard. Don't forget to follow through, and provide them with final receipts, so they can pay the recoverable depreciation. If you don't you are leaving money on the table.

Your policy will specify the time period in which you can submit a claim for this recoverable depreciation. Look at this period closely. It may be 180 days or some other period and will probably say what needs to be done if you need to extend that period. Read your policy and do what it says.

It will be up to you to follow through and submit the receipts for these items when you purchase them. If you don't you might as well kiss this money goodbye. Remember, this can be many thousands of dollars. If you are going to replace the item, then submit the receipt and request your recoverable depreciation. Don't throw away this money! Follow the standard letter format and your item list that accompanied your claim along with the receipt for that item.

If there are numerous disputes or the items are expensive, then you may want to appeal to an appraisal. Having your own appraisal performed can be a strategic and wise thing to do.

If part of your property which is damaged is part of a set, then you may have coverage to replace the entire set.

If your insurance company notifies you that they are going to pay your claim for personal property, then their notice should also state whether they will take all or part of the damaged property as salvage. If there is expense, then the insurance company should bear this expense.

There are basically three actions which can occur for your personal property. These are Replacing, Repairing, Cleaning.

Replacing.

Normally if an item is lost, stolen, damaged and cannot be repaired, or if the cost of repair exceeds the replacement cost. Then your insurance company should pay to replace it.

Repairing.

If an item can be repaired, then your insurance company may suggest repairing it. An experienced repair person should then be consulted who can provide an estimate. If your insurance company wants to repair an item, then have your insurance company send a repairman who can then provide a written estimate. If the insurance company have not done this, then be proactive and find someone qualified and capable of performing the repair. Get a written estimate. If after refinishing, your furniture does not match or look like it did previously, then you can argue for replacement.

Make sure that the item will be warranted. If a pre-existing warranty will be voided, then you could reason with your insurance company that the item needs to be replaced since the pre-existing warranty has been voided and is no longer re-warrantable. Often your insurance company will then elect to replace the item.

Cleaning

Most often this is for items that are washable or can be dry-cleaned. Cleaning will often be enough for clothing however if the item is upholstered furniture, mattress, or box springs be certain that it is certifiably clean. This is especially true if your home has had environmental contamination, such as mold, fungi or smoke. Make sure that not only your air quality is good, but that these items are truly cleaned. If after cleaning, stains or a musty odor remain, then you can notify in your insurance company in writing and request that they replace the item.

Heirlooms and Antiques

Note: If something is an antique, family heirloom or something that cannot be readily purchased, it is important to have a qualified appraiser evaluate the item before it was damaged and also ascribe a price for it after damage. If the insurance company pays you to replace something, then the insurance company has the right to salvage the item. Keep this in mind, especially regarding antiques or family heirlooms. A qualified appraiser can often give you the name of a reputable restoration expert. Contact this person or company and obtain a written estimate for the repair of the specific item. You can then present this to your insurance company. In this way, you can have your antique or heirloom repaired without losing possession of it. The same counsel is true if the item is a work of art.

In regard to works of art, it is wise that the items have special coverage. Antiques, works of art, musical instruments, collectibles etc. should have a rider for scheduled personal property. Hopefully, you will have these coverages in effect at the time of loss.

When submitting a claim for contents the information that is commonly required includes the following: If you don't know everything found below then at least have a written description and photo to document.

Item

Room location

Description

Quantity

Age

Manufacturer/brand

Serial #

Purchase price

Photo #

If the adjuster does not offer you a contents checklist then ask for one. You will need to fill it out completely with requested information.

The easiest way to record this information is to begin in a room and document all the items in that room. If you begin from the ceiling, you can search the items in the room that have been damaged. Take note of furniture legs, upholstered surfaces, electronic devices, wall hangings etc.

Be honest and do not include any items that had preexisting damage or normal wear and tear. Only include items that were damaged because of your loss. Insurance fraud is a crime punishable by the law. Be thorough in your examinations, if your home had water intrusions be certain to look at the bottom of furniture legs.

If you have not yet gone room by room through your house to search for damage you should do it. Have someone with you during this process. They can take a picture of the item and give you the picture number so that you can annotate it.

You will want to have a documentation sheet which has sufficient room for you to list each of your items. I recommend having a different sheet for each room, wherever there has been damage. Please turn to the addendum for a sample content list.

Please visit www.howtosettleyourclaim.com to download free content checklists that you can use for this purpose.

16

Review Your Damages

Let's face it, no one, except for your builder, knows your property as well as you. You have owned it or lived in it for years, maybe even decades. You know what it was like before your loss and you know what it is like now. This chapter will tell you what to do with what you already know.

Why not use this knowledge wisely? Why leave the assessment of your damage to someone who has never seen your home before? Someone who does not know what it looked like before your loss?

To review your loss properly, you will have to use your eyes and make a written record.

The purposes of this record are numerous and its effect is powerful! The suggestions in this chapter are perhaps the most important ones in this book to assist you in settling your claim getting the money you deserve.

Let me call to your remembrance words from the introduction of this book. "Many assume that the insurance company will simply "take care of it", only to find out later that things "did not go as they expected". This chapter will give you very important tools to prevent this from happening to you.

Be honest: Do not list damages which might have been pre-existent to the loss. Don't list normal wear and tear. List only those things which you believe were attributable to your loss event. Nothing more, nothing less. Insurance claim fraud is punishable by law. Excessive, fraudulent claims may also cause premiums to go up, and this hurts everyone.

There are four reasons why you need to create your own written review of damages:

1) For your own peace of mind…

Experiencing a substantial loss to your home or property can be very stressful. Property owners generally feel out of control or at the mercy of someone else, and this adds to their stress. By creating your own review, you will have a better idea of what the damages are and you will have more peace of mind knowing that things have not been overlooked. A detailed review will help you determine whether your claim is being handled accurately and fairly and you will have more of a sense of control!

2) You can provide it to the adjuster when he/she comes

You can give your review notes to the adjuster when he/she arrives and it will assist him/her in correctly itemizing the damage. You will be expediting your claim process by helping to minimize things that the adjuster might overlook

3) If the adjuster has already been to your property....

If the adjuster has already been to your property you can use your estimate as a mirror to hold up to the one that the adjuster or insurance company provides. You can see the things that may have been overlooked and you might also find that the insurance company has found things that you overlooked.

4) When you have a contractor come to your property to estimate damages...

If you are going to have a contractor estimate your damages (a wise thing to do), then the contractor can use your report as a valuable tool to speed his work and ensure that nothing is missed.

Review of Damage Forms:

In the addendum at the end of the book you will find forms that can make your review easy. Use these simple checklists to assist you in creating your own review of damage.

It is not necessary to calculate the square footage, linear length, or actual costs of an item. The adjuster or contractor will do that in preparing his estimate.

As you are preparing your checklist, you should take pictures of this damage for your own files. The addendum has checklists that you can use. Copy them out of the book or you can download the lists for free at www.howtosettleyourclaim.com.

The first checklist is for the outside of your home. Begin with the front of your house and look at the roof and work your way down the structure. Then move to the right side, the left side, and the rear of your home. Finally, look at your lot for additional structures or damage to fences, trees, shrubs, etc.

The four checklists that follow the exterior list are for the various rooms in your home. Don't forget your basement if you have one. You can list this room and any others under "other".

Go into each room of your house.

If possible, begin by going into your attic to look for water staining on your roof decking. Be extremely careful as there may not be floor covering. Make sure someone is with you and knows where you are. I recommend that a roofing professional inspect both your roof and your attic, and you don't do this yourself. Safety first!

If water has come in from your roof, then be sure to examine all ceiling lights, fans, and vents. Also check all outlets and specifically around and under windows if your damage was storm related. An electrician can do this for you. Again remember, Safety first!

Be certain to check your floor coverings for water damage especially around exterior walls or near plumbing leaks or AC Units. Water often will come through these holes, rotting or rusting building materials.

Do not forget to check in your closets.

Do not forget to check under sinks and cabinetry for leaks or water damage

Now, get a clipboard with your lists in hand and go to work documenting damages! Remember this is a crucial step in determining if you should file a claim. These lists (once completed) are also great to give to contractors as they estimate your work. Lastly you want to be able to give this to your adjuster when he/she visits. That way they will have to examine your damages very closely.

You can download at www.howtosettleyourclaim.com

17

The Adjuster Visit: What to Expect.

After the filing of your claim, an adjuster will want to visit your property. When he/ she calls, get your legal pad in your file and write down the adjuster's name and phone number and if possible a cell number. You will want to write this down if you should have to re-schedule or if you find that your adjuster is late for the appointment. Sometimes an adjuster may be late because he/she had to visit a property before yours, and upon arriving at that property there may have been more damage than expected. This may require the adjuster to stay longer and delay your appointment. So, be patient, but get a phone number and write down the date and time.

Before the adjuster arrives complete these 2 steps if possible:

1) Make sure your property is neat, clean and orderly. The adjuster will probably be taking photos... You do not want him/her writing in a report that some of the problems are due to unseemliness or maintenance issues. If your claim should go sour and it becomes necessary to file suit and possibly go to trial, you do not want your dirty laundry being shown up on the witness stand. Although this is only common sense, it is a good reminder.

A True Story

I had a claim in the Dallas, Texas area. There had been numerous water damage events in the home. These damages included three roof leaks from two hail storms, an air conditioning overflow leak, and plumbing leaks at several locations. Because of these numerous damages, there was some significant mold growth appearing in this home and the children were chronically sick. It was this chronic sickness which prompted their doctor to ask if there was mold in the home and cased the eventual filing of the claim. Fortunately, the property owners had coverage for mold in the event of these covered losses.

When testing was performed by an environmental company, the report read that there was significant mold growth and dust in the home. These results were caused by water damage, but also from accumulated dust and dirt. The report said that this probably had the cumulative effect on creating poor air   quality in the home, which contributed to the occupants' poor health. This statement in the environmental report made it more difficult in the settling of this claim since the insurance company took the position that some of the air quality problems were the result of cleaning issues. They were right in this and this presented more challenges to overcome. The claim was eventually settled.

Moral of the story… Keep your home clean and as dust free as possible. It's better for your health and for your home.

2) Walk around the outside of your home and note all the damages. We call this doing your homework! By writing down the damages that you see on the front, right, rear and left side of your home. Be sure to look your roof over. Then look over the inside of your home, beginning with the ceilings, down the walls and to the floors. Use the checklists in this book. These helpful lists describe what to look for, and how to note damages to the exterior and interior of your home. There is even a list for damage to contents.

During the adjusters visit you should:

1) Have an adult family member, neighbor or friend there when the adjuster arrives. Since that person is not named on your insurance policy he should have nothing to say about your claim however it can be helpful to have someone there listening. Having a person there can be of use so that you can more accurately recall what was or was not said during the visit.

2) Be sure to show the adjuster around the exterior and interior of your home, pointing out the damages that you have observed. Then give him/her plenty of space to do their measurements, take photos and annotate the damages. Try not to break your adjuster's concentration by talking too much.

3) Give the adjuster your own damage checklist. More information regarding this can be found in the section entitled: Review your Damages.

This helps to eliminate the adjuster missing things, and will give peace of mind to you later when you have reviewed the adjuster's estimate. You will know if he/she has neglected anything.

4) During the adjuster's visit, he/she may want to interview you as to what happened, or ask other information about your property. Some states permit and some

insurance companies have a policy of taking a recorded statement. The adjuster may ask you if that is okay. If you are interviewed, then simply answer the questions. If you don't understand a question, then ask for clarification. If a question is uncomfortable, then ask the adjuster to re-phrase it. If you don't know the answer, then tell him so. Don't be intimidated. Simply tell the truth as you know it and nothing more. Don't feel like you have to explain a lot, just simply answer the questions if you are able.

5) Ask the adjuster when you can expect to hear back from him/her with an estimate of damages and when a check will be issued. Write this information down in your legal pad. Also, make sure you have the adjuster's phone, fax, cell (if possible) and address. You don't want to lose track of this adjuster. He/she is now the most knowledgeable insurance representative regarding your claim. Future communications should be directed to this adjuster unless you are told otherwise.

When the adjuster leaves you should:

Immediately after the adjuster leaves, write down in a notepad the details of the adjuster's visit. It is a good idea to have a notepad and file strictly for all of your claim information.

What time did he/she arrive and leave? Did he bring anyone like another adjuster or contractor, or assistant? What were their names, and did you get a card?

Here are some other observations that you will want to write down. Did the adjuster walk around the entire house? Did he/she go on the roof? Did the adjuster take pictures? Did he/she go through your home thoroughly? Did he/she write down the damages you pointed out?

Remember, if you are prepared, and have completed your "Damage Checklist", you could give the adjuster a list of damages and their locations. If you are not prepared you run substantial risk. Failure to do this can cause the adjuster to miss things. Then, when he/she completes there estimate you may find that your home has damage that wasn't estimated and paid for by your insurance company.

You don't want this to happen because you will then have only two alternatives:

1) Pay for these damages out of your own pocket. That is not why you pay premiums!

Or,

2) Supplement your claim, which will involve challenging the first adjuster's conclusions, and will quite possible mean that you will find another adjuster assigned to your claim. If your home was affected by a catastrophic situation like a hurricane, tornado, hail storm, or earthquake, it is likely that you will have a cat (catastrophic) claims adjuster. This is someone who may be from another state doing temporary work in your area. It will be hard to follow up with this person, and more than likely your claim will be reassigned. Then, you will be waiting again for the file to be reassigned and another adjuster's visit. This of course will slow the process down, resulting in increased delays and frustration for you. Don't let this happen to you, be prepared and do it right the first time!

18

Understanding Your Adjuster's Estimate

Some people have asked me "How can I know if my home's damages have been properly estimated?"

The answer is, that if you are fully insured…. and your coverage limits are realistic and up to date… and your loss is a covered loss, then, you should have no expense, other than your deductible in restoring your home. You should not have to do the repairs yourself. You should be able to hire professionals. If you cannot do this, then you are either under insured, your claim has not been properly estimated, or you have left money on the table, or because you did not receive your recoverable depreciation and or overhead and profit. If you don't understand this read on. Get what you deserve!

Unless a person is a general contractor, the interpretation of an insurance estimate of repair can be quite daunting. Often the estimate will be accompanied by a brief cover letter and sometimes with a check, usually made out to the insured and your mortgage company, if you have one. There are several issues regarding these estimates that are worth mention.

It takes time to create a good estimate:

The amount of time that elapses between the visit of your adjuster and your receiving his/her estimate for repairs will vary. It depends upon several factors. The first factor is often the workload of the adjuster. If an area has been hit hard by a storm or major event, then the adjuster may have a stack of claims already on his desk. Many adjusters try to work off of a first come, first served basis. Although insurance companies try to spread out the work load for their adjusters, it can become nearly overwhelming if the loss in a geographic area has been severe. The best thing to do is to ask the adjuster when he is at your home, "How long do you think it will be before I will hear back from you with an estimate?" A normal response is usually somewhere between one and three weeks. Take note of the adjuster date and write it down. If you have not received it by that time, then call the adjuster and inquire as to the delay. Don't forget to call.

Once you receive the estimate, you will need to review it!

Before you will really know if an estimate is complete or not, you must do your own homework. If you have used the damage checklist you have already done a thorough walk around the outside and inside of your home and created a checklist of damages, then you can compare it to the insurance company's estimate. Look at the damages found throughout your home. If it looks as if all the issues are covered, then great! However, don't fully assume that this is the case. It is very wise to have a general contractor examine your home or at least a roofing company if your roof has been damaged. This is always a good idea. Of- course doing your homework by creating your list of damages will be helpful to these contractors also!

Since someone is going to have to perform repairs, you should immediately get a licensed contractor to come out and give you a written estimate for repair. It is possible that the contractor might find things that were overlooked by you or the adjuster. You should submit this new information to your insurance company immediately. If there is no new information, then you will at least have a contractor that can perform the work if you so choose.

Concerning the estimate:

Most of the time the insurance company's estimate will be broken down under the following categories:

Additional structures

Exterior

Roof

Debris removal

Interior

Personal contents

Loss of use / Additional living expense

Loss of Use /ALE is usually paid as the expense is incurred. For instance, if you have to move to a hotel, or kennel your pets as a result of your loss, your insurance company will reimburse you, upon providing a receipt. It is important to receive permission before incurring the expense so notify your company/ adjuster of what you will need to do in advance. Review your policy for more details.

It is very important to read your policy because you may have purchased additional coverage and not be aware of it and your adjuster may overlook it. For instance, you might have coverage for a screened porch enclosure, but not know it. I have seen this often in the state of Florida.

You may also have coverage for "loss assessment." If you live in a neighborhood with an association and pay yearly fees, and trees, landscape, fences or common use buildings were destroyed, then your community might want to levy an assessment to get the neighborhood back in order. Your loss assessment coverage might pay for this.

Additional structures may include detached garages, sheds, gazebos or other structures. Your policy will most likely provide further definition of these structures.

Your roof will not only include the roof surface itself, but also the waterproof membrane or underlayment, decking, vents, chimney, flashing and drip edges to name just a few.

Your exterior will be comprised of wall materials, paint, siding, windows, screens, shutters, trim, gutters, doors, porches and many other items. Some rare policies may exclude some exterior paint surfaces. You will need to check your policy.

Debris removal may include removal of trees, shrubs, and wind or water carried debris. If your home is flooded by a leak, then the cleanup may be under debris removal. This coverage also may have separate limits or endorsements.

The interior of your property estimate will most often be broken down room by room. Take your own list of damages that you did as your homework and go room by room to see if the adjuster has missed things. It is quite possible that the adjuster may find some things that you have missed.

Check your deductible.

Your deductible is the amount of money that you must pay in a loss before your insurance company will pay. However, check your policy because some items may have their own deductible. This is sometimes overlooked. If you are satisfied that the adjuster has been thorough, you are not aware of missed items and your damages are below your deductible, then your damages are probably not extensive. However, you will have to pay for these repairs out of your own pocket. Don't delay in getting these repairs done. If you don't do the repairs and the damage gets worse this will only cause more problems. If you later find more extensive damage and want to file a claim, then your insurance company could argue that you failed to mitigate the damages and that it is no longer their responsibility.

If paying your deductible is a huge pill to swallow, then consider visiting with your agent to get a new, lower deductible in case you have a new claim in the future. Generally, the lower the deductible, the higher the premium. You must weigh the risks and consider your own financial situation.

a) Depreciation and Recoverable Depreciation

Depreciation is used to determine the actual cash value of an item. For instance, brand new carpet in your home has a higher value than six-year-old carpet. The same is true for your roof and many other items in your home. You will have to look at your policy to see if you have an ACV policy (Actual Cash Value) or RCV (Replacement Cost Value) policy. Look at your policy and if you are unsure then talk to your agent!

In dealing with a replacement cost policy an adjuster will often total all the damages and then take off recoverable depreciation for some of the items in the property. This recoverable depreciation is then withheld by your insurance company. Although your policy may be for replacement cost, most insurance companies hold this recoverable depreciation until you do the repairs and furnish the receipts.

Once receipts are in hand matching the recoverable depreciation, the insurance company will then reimburse you. Usually when you receive your estimate from the adjuster, a letter will accompany it describing this recoverable depreciation. Don't overlook this amount, as recoverable depreciation can easily be thousands of dollars and you are entitled to it, however you must follow up on this. Don't expect the insurance company to chase you down for receipts so that they can pay you more money. In my years of experience this is a major failing of property owners and as a result much money has been left uncollected from insurance companies. Don't let this happen to you!

It is sad to say, but often time property owners look at the check that they first received and realize that it is not enough to get the work done. They don't understand recoverable depreciation and no one takes the time to explain it to them. So, they try to do repairs themselves to avoid spending more money out of pocket. Don't try to save money. If you hire someone and collect and keep your receipts, you can get that recoverable depreciation! Don't forget this one. Many times, it is worth thousands of dollars to you!

b) Overhead and Profit

This is another one in which people have lost tens of thousands of dollars merely out of ignorance.

If your adjuster's estimate for property damage was estimated at $50,000 for materials and labor but there is no overhead and profit written on the adjuster's estimate, then you would normally be entitled to another $5,000 for overhead and another $5,000.00 for profit. That is $10,000 more dollars that you have received. Some insurance companies routinely put the O&P on the estimate while I have seen others leave it off. If you don't request it, you may not get it. Unfortunately, I have seen that happen.

To qualify for O&P, the repairs to your property usually must include at least three different trade people. That is where the overhead and profit comes in. O&P is to pay the overhead and profit of a General Contractor. General Contractors must estimate your work, provide liability and other insurances, warehouse tools and materials, and select and hire these various trade people. Sometimes they are sub-contractors and sometimes they are directly on the ongoing payroll. These trade people may be roofers, plumbers, electricians, carpenters, painters, heating/AC, landscapers, etc.

Again, I have seen tens of thousands of dollars lost because the property owner thought they didn't have enough money after receiving his/her first check that accompanied the estimate. So, they began to do the work themselves or hired family or a friend down the street. They property owners simply did not understand or were educated in how to obtain overhead & profit. (O&P)

To receive O&P, most insurance companies will require you to provide them with a signed contract with a general contractor. Do this! You can then get typically 20% more than if you did not receive the O&P. You will probably have enough then to hire a qualified contractor and get on with your life!

19

The Difference Between an Insurance Adjuster and A Public Adjuster?

a) Staff Adjuster

A staff adjuster is an employee of an insurance company who serves the interests of his/her employer. In most cases he/she is paid a salary. In order to minimize expenses, some insurance companies are now retaining more independent adjusters and keeping in house or staff adjusters for review of the independent adjusters' claim review. Insurance adjusters are licensed in most states. A staff adjuster usually only works for one company. A staff adjuster may be on a salary or paid per claim handled. He/she will be paid by the insurance company regardless of how much or little you are paid. Always remember that a staff adjuster is working for the interests of his/her employer first and foremost and are paid by the insurance company.

b) Independent Adjuster

An independent adjuster is self-employed or works for an independent adjusting firm that is retained by several insurance companies on a loss-by-loss basis. He/she is usually not kept on salary by any insurance company. It is important to note that it is very likely that you might find another adjuster assigned to your claim if you need to supplement with new information. This is another reason why it is important to try to get the job done correctly to begin with. Independent adjusters are licensed the same as staff adjusters in most states. Independent Adjusters work for insurance companies, and are paid by them regardless of the amount you are paid.

c) Licensed Public Adjuster

A licensed public adjuster is an adjuster retained by you, the policyholder on a loss-by-loss basis. In most states, a special "Public Adjuster" license is required along with bonding.

The public adjuster is not paid by the insurance company. He is paid by the policy holder. This payment is often made as a percentage of the monies that are received from the insurance company. Sometimes these fees may be paid on an hourly basis. Most states have regulations regarding licensing and/or fees and some states do not. The department of insurance in your state stipulates the licensing requirements for training, licensing and bonding of these professionals.

Your public adjuster serves your interests exclusively when dealing with the insurance company's adjusters. Most often, a Public Adjuster will have extensive experience in construction, negotiation, and insurance issues. Since most of the time they work on a contingency basis and are paid for results, (that is, not getting paid till you get paid), they will work diligently to get you the maximum amount. A public adjuster cannot work for an insurance company, they work for you.

Although individual states vary in their description of the duties of a Public Adjuster the following statement is somewhat typical:

"A Public Adjuster can manage your entire claim process. This includes inspection of the loss site, preparing a list of all lost property, calculating a dollar value for your losses, reviewing your policy provisions, assist in your hiring of contractors to make repairs, inspecting the repairs as they are performed, and handling claim paperwork required by the insurance company."

Remember this most important distinction: a public adjuster works for you and not the insurance company!

As the author of this book I can say that I have, and continue to enjoy being a Public Adjuster. Time has not permitted me to serve as many clients as I would like and the need is great so, I have written this book.

The department of insurance in most states can provide a list of licensed Public Adjusters. Care should be taken in the selection of your Public Adjuster since they will work closely with you and your concerns in the settlement of your claim.

20

Loss of Use

If your home has become uninhabitable as a result of the loss and you need to seek other lodging, then these expenses may be covered. If you have this coverage, then your policy should specify its limits. When accessing loss of use keep in mind the amount available and the length of time it is projected to complete repairs. This is especially true if you have had to move out. You do not want to run out of money by spending too much each month or allowing repairs to start or finish late.

You should keep a record of:

> All hotel, or motel charges, apartment expenses
>
> Meal charges
>
> Extra gasoline expenses
>
> Pet kennel charges
>
> Extra phone expenses
>
> Extra utility expenses
>
> Extra/new clothing expenses
>
> Laundry or dry-cleaning expenses
>
> Extra phone expenses
>
> Extra expenses if incurred to re-establish a home office.

If possible, it is good to speak with the adjuster before incurring these expenses. If you had to begin incurring these expenses before an adjuster contacted you, then notify the adjuster as quickly as possible and save all receipts.

Another time that loss of use coverage may be available is during the repair time. If, for instance, your kitchen needs to undergo repairs thereby making cooking impossible or bathrooms are not usable or accessible, or if the house should not be lived in, then your loss of use coverage should cover the expense for alternative accommodations.

If you had to move out of the house, but are considering moving back while waiting for repairs, consider how long the repair process will be. If the repair process will require two months of demolition and repair, but the repairs cannot begin for 90 days, then you will need to make sure that you have enough coverage to take care of these expenses. By this I mean, that if you don't have enough loss of use coverage to sustain you for five months and your personal funds are limited, you might want to move back into the house temporarily (if it is safe) so that you will have enough to pay for your alternative lodging when repairs commence.

In order to calculate these costs, it is wise to make calls for long term accommodations or short-term apartments to estimate these prices. In a geographical area of a major catastrophe (flood, hurricane, twister) it may be very difficult to find accommodations, and they will probably be at full rate.

Loss of use payments are usually made as the cost is incurred. Discuss your accommodations with your adjuster and have his/her approval in writing. Sometimes the insurance company may set up a direct pay with your alternative accommodations, other times they might want to see a signed lease before they will make payment. Make sure that you work with your insurance company and have it all in writing before you proceed.

If you are going to live with family or friends for an extended time, then you must have a lease agreement with them. You must have written legal lease agreement. Submit this lease to your adjuster. It is very important that any lease arrangement be approved by your adjuster and that any monies paid are used for the lease accommodations. Receipts of payment will need to be provided to your adjuster. Failure to do this could result in a denial of the expense payment. Remember, it is wise to get the adjuster's approval of your accommodations in writing. Payment is usually made as soon as expense is occurred. If your rent is due, then it should be made on the due date.

21

Leverage and the Use of Experts

The ancient Greek mathematician Archimedes is reported to have written, "Give me a lever and a place for my feet and I can move the world". Leverage is a key component to success with your claim.

With leverage superhuman feats can be accomplished. The simple scissors lever found in a car jack, can lift a two-ton truck when combined with the simple screw and the turning force of one hand.

The settling of your claim can at times seem like a superhuman task. One reason is that if your home or personal property was damaged then you are probably emotionally affected. Loss of home, property, and comfort can be bringing distress to us emotionally. When we are distressed we are typically at a disadvantage to someone who is calm and/or non-involved. Although your insurance company will probably exhibit a caring attitude, your loss is not a personal loss to your adjuster. You will probably be emotional. It is for this reason that you cannot merely vent off at your adjuster and think that he/she is going to give more money.

If the dispute is not over a coverage issue but rather the extent of damage you may need to hire an expert to create a report. The opinion of an expert enables you to apply significant leverage with your claim.

The type of expert will vary depending on your damages. If you have foundation or structural damage you might need an engineer, electrical damage an electrician, your HVAC an HVAC expert, roof problems a roofing expert. You might have plumbing problems which will require a detailed plumbing inspection or you might have mold or environmental problems requiring an indoor air quality test. Always try to get the best experts possible.

If you need an expert in a field, then call several contractors in that field and ask for the name of an expert who does investigative work. Whatever expert you get you need to ask them what will be the cost for their report. Although an expert might seem expensive, the amount recovered from your insurance company because of this report will usually far exceed the expense. Ask your expert if he has ever been deposed or performed expert witness work and how many times. It is possible that your expert might be challenged by your insurance company and they might want to get another opinion. Make sure that your expert will give you a detailed written report and that he/she is experienced in this type of thing. Your expert might have to one day stand in a trial and give his report and be cross questioned by attorneys. Ask if he will be comfortable with that.

Ask your expert for his/her credentials, review your expert's resume or curriculum vitae. A good expert can be of great worth. Get the best you can afford, while considering the dollar value of your claim. Public Adjusters can usually inform you of quality experts accustomed to providing reports that are substantial and able to provide leverage.

The expert report needs to include a detailed analysis of the damage. The expert must opine if the damage was caused by your filed loss or if it was because of some other reason and why. The report should also include the extent of damages and why it can or cannot be repaired. Does the item(s) need to be replaced? Is it sufficient to repair or must it be replaced? A protocol or repair plan should also be included.

Some experts will want a partial fee to begin and the rest upon completion. If the expert begins an investigation and concludes that the damage is not related to your covered loss, then ask him/her to tell you that early on so that you don't incur the expense of a completed report. The use of a qualified expert can greatly increase the credibility of your claim.

Once a protocol or repair plan has been created, a qualified contractor can than take this report and create a detailed estimate for repair or replacement. Some experts can also clearly define the costs of implementing the repair/replacement plan. Then you can submit all of this to your adjuster.

If an expert opinion is going to be needed it is likely that your insurance adjuster may want to bring one in. On more than one occasion while in dispute with an adjuster over the scope and cost of damages, I have asked for an expert to be retained. I have worked with adjusters to achieve agreement in the expert selection and was then able to get the insurance company to pay for the expert, saving this cost form having to be paid by the property owner. I have used this method in mold expert investigations, smoke and fire damage assessments, content evaluations of damage, and structural damage assessments requiring an engineer's evaluation and repair protocol.

22

How to Supplement Your Claim

If you submit new information on your claim, then you are "supplementing" your claim. If a "final payment" has been issued often a claim is then closed. If a claim has been denied, then the claim will then be closed. In both events you will have to re-open your claim. Do not presume to send your new information to the adjuster that you used to have. Instead, first contact your insurance company and give your claim number to the person on the phone. Say that you have new information that you would like to submit and you need to know to whom and where to send it. The person on the phone may need to get back to you since your claim is closed. Give your information and ask when you should expect to hear back from him. If you don't hear back within couple of days, then call back. Once again give your claim number. Sometimes an insurance company will not re-open a claim until they receive something from you. If that is the case, then send an email or a certified/return letter requesting that the claim be re-opened along with any new information. Include in the letter that you wish an adjuster to contact you ASAP. You should also notify your agent in writing by letter or email.

If you are sending new information, then make sure that you are adequately prepared and know what you are asking for. Are you furnishing an estimate for repair that exceeds what the adjuster has paid? Are you furnishing a letter from your contractor which states that the work is done and final payment needs to be received? Are you furnishing an expert report that proves that damage has occurred which was previously overlooked or denied? If possible, you need to have new estimates in hand that detail the expense to complete the expert's repair recommendations.

There are many reasons to supplement your original claim. Be sure to put all communication in writing.

As a Public Adjuster, I have had to begin my involvement in many claims with supplementation. Usually this occurred because the property owner had received money for the claim, but when the contractor was being selected to do the work, it was discovered that things were overlooked. My services were then sought out and then I went to task proving up the other damages. It is never too late to supplement a claim if the statute of limitations has not passed and the damages can be proven.

23

When Things Are Not Running Smoothly or There is a Dispute

Sometimes you might find yourself in disagreement with your adjuster. Or, you may find that your claim has stalled or feel like you are not being fairly treated. Maybe your claim is proceeding to slowly.

Take the time to read chapter 24, entitled, "Problematic Claims". This chapter details 18 common problems that property owners may face in settling their claim. Strategies to overcome problems are given and you might find the answer to one or more of your problems in the claim illustrations. These strategies can help a derailed claim get back on track.

If, no matter what you do, you can't seem to come to agreement with your insurance company, then you have more options. One option is that if your state permits it, you can hire a public adjuster. (See chapter 19 "The Difference Between An Insurance Adjuster and a Public Adjuster")

Another option is to look in your policy under the section entitled something like "alternative dispute resolution". If you cannot find any information, then contact your state department of insurance. There are several ways in which disputes can be handled. A few options are discussed later in this book they are: mediation (27), arbitration (28) or appraisal (29). The following chapters describe these options more fully. Of course, another option is legal recourse (31) and a chapter is devoted to this topic. Do not allow too much time to elapse in the handling or supplementing of your claim. You do not want the statute of limitations (30) to expire or you will lose your right to file suit.

24

Problematic Claims - Different Types

Once an adjuster has investigated your damages and prepared your estimate, you might find that certain things are excluded. You will need to look at your policy to determine if these exclusions are accurate.

The correspondence that you receive will probably consist of one or more of the following themes:

1. The damages do not exceed your deductible.

2. We are paying your claim minus your deductible or other non-covered issues.

3. We are denying all, or a portion of your claim since there is no coverage.

These are not all of the possible contingencies, but are some of the most common. Hopefully, by this time you would have thoroughly read your policy. If you want specific accurate information regarding your own policy, then you should speak to your agent or your particular state's department of insurance. You may want also to seek the help of an attorney or public adjuster (a public adjuster is someone who specializes in helping property owners settle their claims. In many states, they are required to be licensed).

Now, let's first consider the implications of the three common claims problems listed above, then I will present strategies to overcome 15 more problematic claims that I have encountered.

a) The "Damages are below your deductible" Claim

You will probably receive correspondence including a letter and a brief estimate for repair which states something like this:

"The damages that your home has sustained have been calculated and the total is $_____. This amount is below your deductible of _____. Therefore, no payment will be issued. We regret that we cannot issue payment at this time."

Your letter might differ, but this will give you a general idea of what to expect.

It is possible that your insurance company is accurate in this statement.

Overcoming strategy: The only way to really know whether the adjuster is right being by having created your own checklist (for more details refer to Understanding the Adjuster Estimate). If you have already done a thorough walk around the outside and inside of your home, then you will have a good idea of what needs to be done. Take your damage checklist and compare it to the insurance company's estimate. Look at the damages found on your list, but, don't fully assume that it is correct. Since you are going to have to perform repairs anyway, you should immediately get a licensed general contractor to come out and give you a written estimate for repair. It is possible that the contractor might find things that have been overlooked. You could submit this new information to your insurance company. At the very least, you will have a contractor that can perform the work.

b) The "We are paying your claim minus your deductible or other non-covered issues" claim.

Overcoming strategy: Carefully review your policy regarding coverage and policy exclusions and/or limitations. Be certain that the items mentioned really are excluded. Remember, policies are not a "one size fits all" instrument. Your policy will be different from your neighbor's and it is possible that your insurance adjuster may have overlooked something peculiar to your policy. If, after reading your policy you think that the company is wrong, then you may want to get legal counsel. This is usually wise regarding coverage questions if the interpretation is unclear or seems disputable. Of course, as we have already mentioned, you will want to perform your own inspection to make sure that the amount that they are paying is accurate.

c) The "We are denying all or a portion of your claim since there is not coverage" claim.

Overcoming strategy: As already stated, read your policy. Speak to your agent and/or your state's department of insurance. If you are not satisfied, you may want to seek legal counsel. You will have to weigh the costs of this continued fight, however a knowledgeable attorney can identify if you have a legitimate right and advise you accordingly. If you seek out the help of an attorney, it is good to have your own list of damages available so that the attorney can accurately surmise your case. Once again, having a damage checklist completed will help the attorney.

If you later want to file a claim because you have found more extensive damage, then your insurance company could argue that you failed to mitigate the damages and that it is no longer their responsibility. If paying your deductible is a huge pill to swallow, then consider visiting with your agent to get a new, lower deductible in case you have a new claim in the future. Generally, the lower the deductible, then the higher the premium. You must weigh the risks and consider your own financial situation.

If you feel that the insurance company's estimate has fallen short of what it should be, then you will have to challenge their conclusions. This is not easy, but it can be done.

d) The "There is a dispute over the cost of repairs" claim

Overcoming strategy: If there is a dispute over the cost of repair then you will need to get at least one estimate from a contractor specializing in the repair. If possible, get two or more. Submit the most detailed and accurate to your insurance company. If your adjuster believes that the pricing is too high, then ask where he got his pricing. It is possible that your adjuster is using pricing from a national price list or one that is not specific to your area. Labor costs can vary greatly from city to city and state to state.

Explain to your adjuster that your pricing is from your local contractor who is familiar with the labor cost and material cost in your area. The cost of repairs can increase substantially in an area that is hard hit by a major catastrophe like hurricane or flood. In Florida after the 2004 hurricanes the cost of roofing materials more than doubled in some areas due to the demand for labor and materials. Your local roofer/contractor knows what these prices should be. See if you can schedule a visit between your adjuster and contractor. If your adjuster tells you it is still too much, then tell the adjuster to arrange to have a company come out who will do the work for the adjuster's price. Make sure that you have a written contract for all the work.

e) The "There is a dispute over the extent of damages" claim

Overcoming strategy: If the dispute is not over a coverage issue but rather the extent of damage then you may need to hire an expert to create a report.

The type of expert will vary depending on your damages. If you have foundation or structural damage you might need and engineer, with electrical damage you may need an electrician, with HVAC trouble an HVAC expert, roof problems a roofing expert. You might have plumbing problems which will require a detailed plumbing inspection, or you might have mold or environmental problems requiring an indoor air quality test.

If you need an expert in these fields, then call several contractors in that field and ask for the name of an expert who does investigative work. Whatever expert you get you need to ask them their cost for their report. Although an expert might seem expensive the amount recovered from your insurance company because of this report will usually far exceed the expense.

The expert report needs to include a detailed analysis of the damage. The expert must opine if the damage was caused by your filed loss. The report should also include the extent of damages and why it can or cannot be repaired. Does the item need to be replaced? Is it sufficient to repair or must it be replaced? A protocol or repair plan should also be included. A qualified contractor can than take this report ad create a detailed estimate for repair or replacement.

f) The "Your policy was canceled due to lack of payment" claim

Oops…This one might be fatal!

Overcoming strategy: Look for a canceled check. Make sure that your agent didn't somehow lose it or that your mortgage company failed to pay. If they did fail to do so, then you may have recourse against them… You will probably need an attorney to resolve this matter if it can be solved at all. Most policies require a certain notice period of time before cancellation. If you were not notified you may have some recourse.

g) The "condition existed before you owned the home" claim.

This means that the insurance company believes that the problem existed before your policy took effect. This is most commonly found in a property which has been recently purchased and is newly insured.

Overcoming strategy #1: Your claim was filed at the date of discovery. You may have to furnish your home inspection report or an appraisal report. If your property had a "clean bill of health" it will be harder for your insurance company to resist your evidence.

Overcoming strategy #2: Related to this problem is the issue of the previous owner. If the previous owner intentionally covered the problem or knew of it and failed to disclose it, you may have legal recourse against the seller, agent, broker, or home inspector. Remember, these people also have insurance. You will probably need an attorney to address these other parties.

A True Story

I had this happen on a claim in which the homeowners in San Antonio, Texas purchased a large, three-story , beautiful, historic home. They had been the proud owners for two months. They were doing some remodeling as their aged parents were going to be moving in with them. This family was removing the traditional bathtub to replace it with a step-in shower and hand grips.

During the remodeling, it was discovered that there had been a plumbing leak going on for a long time and that it had caused substantial damage on several floors, in excess of $100,000.00. The insurance company at first denied the claim, but we persisted, stating that the homeowner was unaware, and that no inspector had caught the problem either. The insurance company started to investigate the previous owner who claimed that he had no knowledge of the problem. The insurance company then found (to their surprise) that the previous owner had the same insurance company as the new owner. So, the insurance company took responsibility for the damage, and eventually paid the claim.

h) The "damage did not occur under your current policy" claim

You recently changed insurance companies and your current insurance believes that it happened under the watch of another insurance company.

Overcoming strategy: You can state that your current insurance company had the opportunity to inspect as part of their policy writing process. The insurance company should have discovered and documented the damage at the time of writing the policy. Defend yourself and state that you did not know about the damage until the date of loss. Of-course this is only defensible if you are telling the truth! If you have new insurance because you recently refinanced, then you may have had an inspector or appraiser visit your home so you could obtain the mortgage. If that is the case, then submit the inspector/appraiser's report.

i) This "damage was pre-existing" claim

You file your claim and there is damage, but the insurance company does not believe that it was related to the event which is your covered loss. They think that it was pre-existing.

Overcoming strategy: Did you paint or wallpaper last year, only to find as a result of your recent catastrophe that your walls now have cracks or are discolored? This might prove sudden damage as a result of a loss which would be covered.

A True Story

I once had a claim on the Treasure Coast of Florida in which a house had a cracked slab and had shifted about seven inches. The homeowner stated that the movement occurred because of the hurricane. There were numerous cracks in the walls and tears in the sheetrock tape where the walls met the ceiling. The doors would no longer close properly and some doors would even swing of their own accord. There was a crack in the slab and several floor tiles had popped up, but the homeowner knew that his home did not have these damages before the storm.

Looking at the house it was hard to tell how long the cracks had been there because it had been over five years since being painted. Fortunately, the homeowner was in the process of refinancing his home just a few weeks before the hurricane did occur. As part of the refinancing process, an appraiser had visited his home, taking pictures just a couple of weeks before. We submitted the appraiser's report and pictures which indicated no cracks or foundation damage. The insurance company decided to settle the claim paying the policy limits since the damage was related to the hurricane.

Moral of the story: If you believe that the damage occurred because of the loss, then look for documentation that supports that the damage occurred suddenly as a result of the loss. You may find proof in photos or in recent reports for financing, or new paint or wallpaper, or flooring that was damaged.

j) The "Lost" claim

The insurance company says that they have no record of your having filed a claim.

Overcoming strategy: Are you sure that you filed your claim?

If the answer is yes, then how did you file it? Did you call it in? If you did, then reconstruct what you did to call the claim in. Did you call your agent? Who did you speak to? Did the agent say that he/she would call your claim in for you? Contact your agent and see if there are any notes in your file referencing your call regarding the claim. If you filed your claim by letter, then of course you should be able to produce this letter to your insurance company.

k) The "We're going to fix it…. then we change our mind" claim.

Overcoming strategy: This is a difficult claim to overturn because it depends upon the documentation that is present. I recommend that if you have a meeting with the adjuster and the adjuster makes statements or promises to you, that you write these statements down immediately. In the chapter of this book entitled "The Adjusters' Visit: What to Expect", I go into detail regarding the adjuster's visit. Write down in your legal pad any statements of coverage or promises made. Be as accurate as possible. If you had a family member or friend there with you, then have that person help you recall what was said. After the adjuster has left, it is good to send a letter (see correspondence chapter) to the insurance company. In this letter reaffirm the statements of the adjuster using the adjuster's own words. In your letter quote the statements that you and your witness recall the adjuster saying to you. If the adjuster gave you a time when the estimate would be prepared, then quote that time and state that you are looking forward to his/her response. Send this letter ASAP to the adjuster. If you fax it, make sure that you keep a copy of your fax report. If it was emailed then keep all emails in a separate folder with this letter in hand, it becomes more difficult for the adjuster to forget statements that were made or to go back on his/her word.

If another adjuster becomes assigned, then he/she will have your correspondence in the file confirming the statements of the first adjuster. The second adjuster will often then build the report off the information in the file. This adjuster will see your letter and must take those statements into consideration. It is great if the second adjuster agrees with these records, but if he/she disagrees, then you are entitled to clear explanations as to why the first adjuster is considered to be wrong.

If the first adjuster affirms coverage for a loss, then it makes it more difficult for a second to deny coverage. Contradictory behavior may lead to bad faith issues with your claim. If you feel you that have been deceived or that the story from your adjuster changes, then you may need to seek legal counsel. If this is the case, you will be glad that you had written this letter affirming your adjuster's conversation with you.

l) The "You don't meet the deductible" claim.

Overcoming strategy: The best way to determine if you meet the deductible is to do your own damage checklist. Survey the exterior and interior. Make detailed notes of all damages. Then, call a general contractor and or roofer etc. (you will need to have the repairs done anyway). If your contractors estimate exceeds your deductible, then provide your adjuster with this new information. If not, then complete repairs.

Take your own list, go room by room to see if the adjuster has missed things. It might also be possible that the adjuster has found things that you missed. If you are satisfied that the adjuster has been thorough, you are not aware of missed items and your damages are below your deductible, then your damages are not so extensive. That is great, however you will have to pay for these repairs out of your own pocket! Don't delay in getting these repairs done. If you don't do the repairs and the damage gets worse, this could cause you trouble in the future.

m) The "Partial coverage" claim.

Under this claim your adjuster might say some items may be covered while other items are not.

Overcoming strategy: Pay close attention on this issue and read your policy. Mold might not be covered but water damage will. You may have lost items or things in your house. Were they a part of a set that cannot be replaced? Then you may be able to get the whole set replaced since most policies have coverage for sets.

Review chapter 12 of this book. It is possible that your loss was an indirect or consequential loss. If so you might have coverage.

n) The "I'll take care of you…. and later do nothing" claim.

Overcoming strategy: If you took notes during the adjusters visit as recommended in the chapter entitled "The adjusters visit what to expect" you should be in good shape. If you did not send a confirmation letter at that time, then send it immediately. Be sure to mention the names of any witnesses that were present at the time and give the direct quotes as to what was said.

If the adjuster begins to tell you something different on the phone, then ask him/her to put it in writing and send this to you. At that time, you will then have a written record of two contradictory statements. You can then ask for a supervisor's name and forward both letters to the supervisor. Hopefully the situation will then be resolved. If the dispute is over the extent of damages, then you might need to get additional estimates proving the extent of damage and cost of repair. These can then be forwarded to your adjuster.

o) The "Forever" claim.

This is the claim that never seems to move forward.

Overcoming strategy: Change your approach. If you have been making phone calls then begin to fax and send emails or mail letters. If you are getting no response, then ask for a supervisor's name and address and send a letter or email detailing the delays to the supervisor. Copy the supervisor and your insurance agent on emails. If writing letters, be sure to send this certified/return receipt. Ask for a response within five business days and tell the supervisor that you will be filing a letter of complaint with the state board of insurance if no response is forthcoming. If there is no response, then send a letter to supervisor and to your state.

p) The "They keep changing adjusters" claim

Some insurance companies do this routinely while others try to keep the same adjuster on the file. There can be many reasons for this. One factor has to do with the workload of the adjusters. Sometimes files will be reassigned to lighten the load. Other times it might be simply that the adjuster quit. However, this is quite commonplace. You will usually find a new adjuster assigned if payment has been issued and then you re-open or supplement your claim with new information.

Overcoming strategy: If you have been keeping good records you should be in good shape. You should have letters confirming any conversations or promises.

It is possible that the new adjuster may want to visit your property. This is especially true if you are challenging the first adjuster's estimate and providing new information. Remember, every adjuster has a boss to whom he/she may have to justify his/her position. Give the adjuster plenty of documentation for your claim.

q) The "They don't return my phone calls" claim

Overcoming strategy: Realize that sometimes an adjuster might be overloaded or be waiting for more information. Try to be patient. However, if you think that you are being ignored, then stop making phone calls and send a letter certified/return or start sending faxes (be sure to keep a fax record- see Correspondence). Send an email to the adjuster and send a copy to a supervisor. If after several attempts you are still getting no response send copies of this correspondence to your states dept. of insurance and file a complaint. Send a copy of your complaint to the insurance company.

r) The "Check is in the mail" claim

Overcoming strategy: If a check has been promised and it has not yet been received, call the adjuster and ask him/her to check the address that it was sent to. Was it sent to the property address? Are you living at the property now? Perhaps it was sent to the wrong address. If it was sent to the right address and you still have not received it after a couple weeks, then you may need to call the adjuster and have a stop payment issued. Be sure to ask where the check was being sent from. Sometimes a check request from an adjuster can take a week to be completed by a corporate office.

Believe it or not: Be sure to check with your spouse or family members regarding any mail that has come in. More than once I have had a spouse endorse and deposit a check without the other spouse knowing about it. Perhaps a family member set aside the mail and forgot to tell you. Ask around.

25

Dealing with Your Mortgage Company

If you have received money for an insurance claim for your property it may have your mortgage company's name affixed to the check. The reason for this is at the time of your insurance policy initiation or renewal your mortgage company loan was in effect. If that is the case, here are a few things that are important to be aware of, as you seek to process the funds for repairs:

- Remember, your mortgage company is part owner of your property. They will continue to be so until the mortgage note is paid off. It is important to maintain their trust. By trying to follow their procedures you will most likely be able to gain their cooperation in the fastest manner possible.

- Keep in mind, as part owner they will want to make sure that the value of the property is maintained. Unfortunately, in the past some unscrupulous property owners have had claims where they collected the money without making any repairs to the property. This behavior diminishes the property value. As a result, if a mortgage company ever had to foreclose on the property then they are left in the bad position of owning a property whose value has diminished. It is understandable that there are some procedures in place to protect their investment.

Here are some things to consider:

- If a mortgage proceed is smaller in amount, say under fifteen thousand dollars or so, some mortgage companies may simply sign the check and return to the insured. If that is the case, you should take the check to the mortgage lender for signature. After the mortgage lender has endorsed the check then you should sign.

- If you have received a check requiring the mortgage lender's endorsement, then you should call your mortgage lender. It is important to have your mortgage loan number or the owner's social security number available by which the insurance company can confirm the loan number.

- Your mortgage loan number will be your identifying number in all communique with your mortgage company.

- Your mortgage company will not be following your insurance claim number, so don't expect them to have your insurance claim number. Always refer to your mortgage loan number when speaking to your mortgage company.

Note: Some mortgages might have changed hands since you first originated your loan. Loans are often sold to mortgage buyers. Whoever you have been making mortgage payments to most recently is the institution you should be contacting. There is a possibility that your insurance company may have an old mortgage company as co-payee. If that is the case, you will have to provide a statement showing that the old company is no longer on the mortgage note and present documentation regarding the new loan. I have seen this happen when people have re-financed their mortgage. So, pay attention to who the lender is listed as on your policy.

- IS your mortgage paid off? It is possible if this was done recently that the insurance company may not have been notified, if that is the case, provide your agent and company with statement of payoff.

On your initial call to the mortgage company, you should be prepared:

- Phone your mortgage company and ask for their "Claims Department". Depending on the size of the mortgage company, they may or may not have an automatic answering system. This system may have a "claims dept." which you can press a number # for. If you end up talking to a live person tell them that you "have had an insurance claim and that the mortgage company is one of the names on the check and that you need to have it processed." That person should be able to refer you to the right department to speak with. This will begin the claim file, within your mortgage company.

- At that time, they will ask you a number of questions regarding the claim. Your mortgage company will want to know the amount of the check and the "type" of damage (fire, water, wind, hail, etc.) They will want to confirm your mailing address to furnish you with a packet, or they may want to have you come into a local branch or office. Make sure you give them your correct mailing address as it may differ from the property address of the damaged property.

- It is also a very good idea to make sure that your mortgage lender has your current best cell phone number and email address, as these also may have changed since you first originated your loan.

As previously mentioned, you may be asked or instructed to come into your local lender office, especially, if it is a small check for signing.

If it is a larger check, then you will have to go through a process. There are no hard and fast rules to this process but there are some commonly practiced procedures. They can be demanding so don't take it personal. It's just business.

The mortgage company will want from you:

1) To fully go through the mortgage packet forms and complete all information.

2) The endorsed check.

3) An estimate of repair / adjuster's worksheet (This should have been provided to you by your insurance company, at the time of check issue.)

4) A statement as to your selected contractor for repairs.

5) A written contract with that contractor stating the scope and dollar value of the work.

In addition, many mortgage companies may require the following from your selected contractor: (Some of these requirements may vary according to the mortgage lender and state laws.)

- A copy of the contractor's license.

- Proof of worker's compensation for employees. (varies in each state or city/county)

- Proof of liability insurance of contractor.

- If the job is large (for example: exceeding $200,000.00) proof of financial stability or a performance bond for a specified amount may also be required. (Different states have different laws and financial guidelines)

- Promise of a signed "lien waiver or release" upon payment.

- There may be additional items requested. The contractor requirements will be in your packet. Your contractor should provide all requested information for you to send in, in a timely manner.

May I offer some hard-learned advice? Watch how your contractor handles provision of this information. This may be a good indication as to what to expect from him/her. Make sure your contractor delivers it to you in a timely manner. Your contractor should not complain or delay. Excellent companies provide these items all the time and are ready to deliver quickly.

Sometimes it can be helpful to expedite the claim if the contractor leads the way in communicating with the mortgage company once work has begun. This can help you as the property owner be relieved of being the middle man.

If you want your contractor to be able to communicate with your mortgage company claim department, you will have to sign a release authorizing the designated contractor representative to communicate. You of course should be copied in all communication.

If your insurance company is going to retain the funds and disperse them, here a few tips for success to avoid frustration:

- Always ask for the name and (phone number extension, in case you're disconnected) of the person you're talking to and write it down.

- Don't assume that if you're told something it will always be done as said. Ask for email confirmation of discussed items. Have an email backup, this also gives you something to send to a supervisor if necessary.

- Once all requested information has been submitted and approved you will be ready to proceed. If more info. is requested try to provide it quickly.

- Ask for the name, phone number, email and fax number of a contact person for your claim for future correspondence. (Ask if there is separate file or transaction number, or if loan number is sufficient)

Most mortgage lenders (especially nationwide lenders) have a special office specifically for claim handling. Many mortgage companies now outsource this work to claim administrators that handle the claim processing, you may not be aware of it though. Typically, these offices might even be in another state from where you issue your mortgage payment.

Once initiated, most mortgage companies now maintain a virtual file on you that can be accessed by any person in the mortgage claim department. This means you do not necessarily need to speak with the same person each time, as all files are maintained electronically.

Considering all of this, remember, it is always wise to get that all important email confirmation from the person with whom you last spoke.

Regarding disbursement of funds:

- Draws:

In most larger claim situations, funds will be dispersed on a "draw" basis. You most likely will not get all funds released immediately to you and the contractor. This is because your mortgage company is seeking to protect its asset in your property. They want to make sure all work that is paid for is performed, and that the work allocated in the insurance claim estimate is carried out.

- Inspections followed by draws:

In most cases the mortgage company will want at least two inspections performed (by their own paid inspector). These will typically be at the halfway point of the job and at the end. Some mortgage companies may want to inspect before each commensurate draw is issued. It is important that this is understood and in writing before work commences.

Listen closely to what I am going to say now. Your contractor needs to be good with the draw arrangement. You don't want your contractor stopping work because he/she did not receive enough on a draw. You don't want the contractor, asking you for money personally to stay on the job. Make sure the contractor has agreed to the draw. Talk to him about it! Get it in writing. If he is not comfortable, have him speak with the mortgage company to explain why. If the contractor is not able to live with the draw, DO NOT use that contractor.

On some claims, the draw arrangement with the mortgage company might need to be modified simply because there might be greater costs of demolition, or a need for materials early in the construction process. YOUR contractor needs to discuss this with you and your mortgage company.

Schedule the work and inspection:

It will be up to your contractor to keep the work on schedule. Requests for inspection from the mortgage company and waiting for a draw will require time. This must be understood and a WISE contractor will schedule the work appropriately so that unnecessary delays can be prevented. Your contractor must understand that providing advanced notice to the mortgage company of when they will be ready for inspection is important, as is being prepared for that inspection. WATCH closely how your contractor is performing. As I said before, you will have to authorize the contractor's communication with the mortgage company. By authorizing him to communicate, the burden is upon him to do so. But remember, stay in the communication loop.

Draw amounts:

Different mortgage companies have different policies and the type of work may require some amendments to be negotiated. Your contractor can and should advise.

Some common arrangements are 30% /30% /30% and 10% percent at completion. Another arrangement is 33%/33% and 34% at completion. It is important that the draw percentage and amount of work that needs to be completed before each draw is understood by all involved meaning; you, your contractor and your mortgage company.

Last, but not least…

For your own sake and peace of mind, and for your contractor, consider the following:

As the property owner; YOU will be requested, to make major decisions on items such as flooring, cabinetry, lighting and roofing. Don't cause delays in the process by failing to make those decisions. Get started early, and make your selections quickly and firmly. These items need to be ordered and may take many weeks to arrive. Don't slow everyone down because of your own indecision

26

Selecting a Contractor

Few things are as important as the selection of a contractor in getting your property restored. In a few moments, I will give you a checklist of things to discuss with any contractor that you would consider hiring. But first, let me give you a few warnings especially if you have experienced a loss like a hurricane or flood, or hail storm. Losses of these type can impact tens of thousands of properties at once in a community. Because of this the normal number of contractors serving that community on a regular basis may quickly become overwhelmed with the volume of work.

At the same time, ambitious and opportunistic companies may suddenly come into an area marketing their services. Although many companies are reputable, and suited to "setting up shop" in a community for a year or more, some unfortunately are not. Here are some good questions to ask and make sure you get all the answers.

Where is your office located? Address, Phone numbers

How long have they been doing this type of work?

What is their license number, home state and county??

Tell me about your contracting experience

DO you have a website? What is the URL? This is important! Once you know the website and company name go on line and research. Search for any reviews of the company and read them, especially if they are negative reviews, look for the good, bad and ugly. Check the Better Business Bureau.

May I have a brochure, business card and other literature?

How many employees do you have?

How large is your average project?

May I have a list of previous clients in the area?

How many other projects do you have going on in the area?

How long have they worked with their sub-contractors?

Please read this closely! ALWAYS have a signed contract with all names, phone numbers and addresses. ALWAYS have a specified price and description of all services that will be rendered. NEVER give all of your insurance money to your contractor up front. NEVER pay by cash. ALWAYS get a receipt. The contractor may require a down payment or deposit, but it should be minimal. Once the work is about to begin money can be issued as agreed upon. Some naïve people have been taken advantage of and scammed by unscrupulous individuals or shady companies, so follow my advice and do your homework above.

If for some reason, contractors look at your insurance claim proceeds and believe your claim is underpaid then contact a public adjuster to assess your situation. Some contractors think they can adjust your claim. This is illegal in many states. Contractors cannot legally adjust claims. It is a conflict of interest.

The following questionnaire / statements of information should be used when seeking to choose a contractor. ALWAYS seek the most qualified and skilled and reputable contractor that is available. Don't try to save money by being cheap. Hiring family members or friends is risky as they may not follow through. A well-adjusted and paid insurance claim should provide sufficient money to hire professionals. The best contractors will have no objection to the following questionnaire and will be impressed by your business acumen.

Suggested questions to aid in contractor selection.

The following is requested to help ensure a success repair/renovation project
These are requirements for the consideration of the job. Please answer thoroughly.

A) How long has contractor been in business?
B) Describe diversity of projects completed in past? (including the dollar value and size of projects)
C) How long have you worked with the subcontractors that might be used for this job? (describe their experience)
D) Can you provide me pictures and/or schedule me to visit previous jobs?
E) Are their people that are satisfied clients that I can personally talk to? Name/ Phone #_____ Name / Phone # _____
F) Will you provide me "proof of full payment made to all subcontractors," upon completion of sub-contractor's work?
G) Will you adhere to all the estimate items for repair unless otherwise indicated by the property owner in addendum of contract?
H) **Will you comply with specific materials and grade of products to be installed and purchased as stated in estimate?** (Masonry, lighting, floor coverings, window treatments, paint and wall finishes will be selected by homeowner (in consultation with contractor) within estimated costs of estimate) Any desired changes/upgrades incurring additional costs will be paid for by property owner with signed change order.
I) Will you provide me a copy of insurances? Workers comp. if required?
J) What measures will be taken provide for my safety and security of home and property?
K) A clear **start date** of _____ and projected **completion date** _____.
L) An agreed payment schedule will be_____% _____% _____%.
M) An agreed upon contract will be signed by contractor and property owner, which details payments to be made and specific tasks to be performed.

Signed Property owner: _____ __/__/__
Signed Contractor: _____ __/__/__

27

Mediation

Mediation is one of several alternatives in settling a claim. Most mediations are non-binding, that is, that neither side has the power of the courts to enforce the settlement. Occasionally, a mediation can be binding/non-binding, meaning that it may be binding on the part of the insurance company but non-binding on the part of the insured. This is often the best option for the insured. If you are going to mediation I strongly suggest that you have a public adjuster or attorney assist you. The Public Adjuster can make sure that all of your damages are fully documented.

In mediation, a neutral negotiator helps both sides to come to a settlement. Different states handle this in different ways. Sometimes the expense of the mediator is born equally by both parties. Other times it may be paid by the insurance company alone. Be certain to inquire about the cost.

It is good to find out information about the mediator. Since the mediator is neutral, you should have a say in the mediator selection if your state permits it. Call the mediator's office and ask for a brochure and if there is a website to visit. Read the brochure or go online and research the mediator's background, expertise and the type of mediations that he/she has been involved with. Many mediators are attorneys, or sometimes even retired judges. Make sure that your mediator has experience in mediating property damage issues.

Most mediation times run anywhere from one half to full day mediations, and the cost of these sessions will vary. Unless your claim is exceedingly complicated, you can expect it to run a half day either in the morning or in the afternoon.

In mediation, it is very important that you have strong information to strengthen your case with the insurance company. When you attend the mediation, you should bring written estimates for repair and documentation that supports your claims. Do everything in your power to have strong experts and established companies in providing the estimates. If you think that it will help, it may be advantageous to you to have one of your estimators or experts with you. This is, of course, if he/she is well spoken and professional.

Claim settlement can be an emotional process. This is particularly true since you, the property owner, are emotionally attached to your property. The insurance company understandably does not have the same emotional attachment. Not everyone has the personality or disposition to effectively go through a mediation alone. If you feel this way, you may want to consider retaining an attorney or hiring a public adjuster to assist you in this process. Usually they can be retained on an hourly basis or for a flat fee. It may be helpful to have a family member or someone experienced in negotiation go with you. Once again, I recommend having a Public Adjuster assist as they are often more experienced in this type of negotiation. An attorney is also a viable option.

Before going to mediation, it is important to know how low you can go. What is the bottom line dollar figure that you need to restore your property? Start as high as possible. These numbers must be substantiated by your estimates.

If you feel that there have been claim handling problems with your insurance company, you may want to consult with an attorney beforehand. If you have thoroughly read your policy as we have recommended, you should have some idea if there have been any violations. If you believe that you have been treated unfairly, then you should consult with an attorney.

During the mediation process the mediator will meet with both parties. Sometimes there may be a joint meeting where both sides express their views. Other times the sides may never meet together. If you believe that you have to speak to the other side, then ask the mediator to do so. Listen to the mediator as he/she is there representing your best interests also.

After the initial joint meeting, if there is one, you the insured and the insurance company's representatives will be separated and the mediator will go back and forth from room to room. He may try to talk you down in your demands and comment on the strength of your claim. At the same time, the mediator should be talking to the insurance company about the additional risks and expenses that will occur if they do not settle the claim during the mediation. Try to have as much confidence in the mediator as possible.

Sometimes in mediation you may find the initial demands and first few negotiation volleys to be worlds apart. Don't become too alarmed. This is very common. Try to hold your ground and justify your position by your expert reports and estimates. Let the mediator do his job.

If the attempt at mediation has failed, that is, that you and your insurance company have not been able to find mutual settlement ground, then you must seek alternative solutions. You will then, in most cases, have the option of filing suit, the option of appraisal or possibly arbitration. You should consider these options beforehand. A good thing to do is to discuss these options with your mediator. Of course, if you have retained legal counsel, your attorney can advise you also. Your attorney and or mediator can inform you as to the challenges and risks of each of these alternatives.

28

Arbitration

Some insurance companies have joined an arbitration council in order to stay out of court and to save defense costs. Arbitration councils may be made up of insurance professionals, and may look at the various aspects of the loss and render a decision as to who is at fault and for how much. As is found with many mediators, the arbitrator may also be an attorney, retired judge or other trained professional.

In an arbitration both sides (you, the insured and your insurance company) will present their documentation and perspective to the arbitrator. The arbitrator will then give his/her decision (usually later) as to who is at fault how much the damages will be.

Usually, the best scenario is a binding/non-binding arbitration. That means that the decision of the arbitrator is binding on the insurance company, but non-binding on you, the insured. This leaves you with the option of filing suit if you do not like the arbitrator's judgment.

Occasionally, to increase the general credibility of the arbitral process and to help ensure effective arbitration, arbitrators will sit as a panel which usually consists of three arbitrators. Often the three arbitrators consist of an expert in the legal area of insurance code within which the dispute falls, an expert in the construction industry, and an experienced arbitrator.

Remember though, that there will be risks if your claim goes to trial and there will be additional time waiting for the legal process. Again, with arbitration, as in mediation, you may want to consider retaining a public adjuster to assist you, if an attorney is warranted then the licensed public adjuster will usually recommend it. I do not recommend representing yourself alone at this point in your claim, there are too many factors to consider and you will want the experience that a public adjuster or attorney can provide, especially because you will undoubtedly be emotionally involved.

29

Appraisal

The appraisal process is usually described clearly in the conditions of your insurance policy. It is important to review your policy. If you have questions regarding appraisal speak with your agent or your adjuster. You might also want to consider speaking with an attorney or public adjuster in this regard. In the appraisal process an outside disinterested party with expertise in the construction process and damages is called to evaluate the loss and determine the value of the loss. The appraiser cannot resolve issues about law or coverage.

It is important to note that if the insurance company has one scope of damages and you, the insured, has another scope of damage, then you will probably have problems with the appraisal being successful. Appraisals are most successful when there is no dispute as to the legitimacy of a covered loss or the extent of damages, but only when the cost of repair is in dispute.

If you are considering the appraisal process, then it is important that you have confidence in the appraiser. Ask for a brochure or look at his/her website. Interview the appraiser as to his knowledge of your type of damage. If you are uncomfortable then say so, and seek out another appraiser. It is recommended that you have some assistance in selecting an appraisal representative. An experienced licensed public adjuster is often an excellent choice to help in representation or in the selection of a representative. You may also want to get legal counsel on this selection.

30

Statute of Limitations

Review your policy definitions to determine the statute of limitations. If necessary, obtain legal counsel. Each state has its own laws in effect to this regard. The statute of limitations is usually defined as the period which occurs from the time of loss up to the maximum time to bring a lawsuit against a third party. Sometimes the statute of limitations period begins to run after the investigation and denial of coverage for a claim. Sometimes it may run from the point of discovery of a covered loss. For instance, a hail damaged roof might go unnoticed until discoloration appears on a ceiling several months later. If you did not file a claim after the hail, thinking that your roof was undamaged or you were unaware of the damage until a later time, then the statute may begin to run at the time of discovery. In any case, do not delay in ever filing a claim, especially if more damage will result by failure to repair the damage.

Statutes of limitation differ from state to state and your policy. You must review your policy!

If the date of statute of limitations is approaching since your date of loss, do not hesitate to begin the lawsuit process. Find a competent attorney and file a lawsuit. This will take time. Try to give the attorney at least a few weeks. If you do not do this and the state of limitations period expires, you will likely lose your right to file a lawsuit, and have no further recourse.

It is not the purpose of this book to give legal advice. Consult with an attorney!

31

Legal Recourse

It is unfortunate to say that some claims cannot be settled without legal recourse.

A common reason why a claim may not be settled without legal counsel is that there is a dispute regarding coverage. If your insurance adjuster tells you that you do not have coverage, yet you have read your policy and believe that you do, then you need to consult with an attorney knowledgeable with your type of claim. Not all attorneys are knowledgeable with property insurance and the multitude of issues surrounding this type of claim. Look for someone who specializes in these type of issues and has a successful track record.

One common dispute regarding coverage may have to do with the issue of mold. While a policy may say "we do not cover losses form fungi, rot, rust, mold, etc.", it can sometimes be argued that this type of damage is an ensuing loss, or the result of a covered loss. For instance, if your roof is damaged and water gets inside your wall, it may result in mold growth. It may be possible that you have coverage. The different legal systems in each state have set precedents and different policies deal with these issues in distinct ways. You will probably need to consult with a knowledgeable attorney in your own state.

Another issue has to do with bad faith. If you do not believe that your insurance company is living up to its contract with you in its policy, then there may be issues of bad faith. In your individual policy, their will most likely be stipulations as to how long your insurance company must respond to your claim, send an adjuster, issue payment, send a denial, etc. If these agreements have been violated, you may have legal recourse. It is not within the scope of this book to provide legal counsel.

Remember, if your claim is one that may have occurred due to a catastrophe such as a hurricane, flood, wildfire or earthquake, then you may be one of many thousands of claimants at one time. Sometimes your own state's department of insurance may relax these time deadlines to give insurance companies time to respond to the multitude of claims. It is a good idea to log on to your state's department of insurance website to determine if normal guidelines have been extended or altered.

Another issue, which could possibly arise must do with violation of your individual states deceptive trade practice laws or violations of the Uniform Deceptive Trade Practices Act. You should talk with a knowledgeable attorney to determine if he/she believes that there have been violations.

Regarding legal recourse, it is vital that you keep good records of your claim. Remember in the beginning of the book I said that the most important chapter was chapter #5 which had to do with documentation? If you have been keeping good records you will be glad that you did. An attorney will want these records.

There are many types of contractual agreements with attorneys. Some attorneys want all the money up front, some want a retainer and will bill hourly as work is done and others will take the case on a contingency basis, waiting to be paid when the claim is finally settled. There may also be other ways of retaining legal counsel. You will have to decide the benefits of each.

Personally, I have always been partial to the attorney that will take the claim on contingency, and this is for several reasons. First, he/she will be motivated to get the claim done quickly so they can get paid. Second, they will seek for a higher settlement amount since his/her pay is directly affected. Thirdly, if taken on a contingency basis the attorney will usually have a high confidence and level of success, resulting from previous cases that he/she successfully represented, otherwise they would not normally risk their expenditure of time.

However, this is an individual choice and again, I need to say, I am not attempting to give legal counsel. Each method has its own benefits which should be discussed with your attorney. Public Adjusters can often refer you to attorneys that specialize in this type of work, since they work often with legal counsel and are called upon sometimes as expert witnesses. Most importantly work with an attorney experienced in plaintiff work with insurance companies in construction.

A Note from the Author

Thank you so much for purchasing this book!

I would like to invite you to visit our website for information and to download checklists. www.howtosettleyourclaim.com If your claim is more than $30,000.00, then I would suggest professional consultation with a public adjuster.

We hope you found this book to be informative, practical and helpful. It is truly my desire to help home property owners be relieved of the mental anguish, financial burden, stress, and questions that arise during a property loss.

The unexpected damage and inconveniences which accompany a loss can certainly take its toll on family life which can result in an emotionally stressful environment. It can become a very difficult time for moms, dads and kids. This is also a concern of mine. We want to help.

 If you have a business that has been damaged, get help so you that you don't have to try to manage your business on top of an insurance claim. A public adjuster can help you do that.

If you don't have an insurance claim now, that is great. The information shared in these pages will serve you well in any type of insurance claim that you or a family member might experience in the future.

Perhaps in your future there will be someone that needs the help this book offers, and you can help. If so, please pass your information along.

For more information, helpful videos, and other insurance claim guidance and support visit: www.RLCarterAdjuster.com.

To order more books and download damage checklists, visit:

www.HowTo SettleYourClaim.com

Best wishes on your claim,

Rick Carter - Public Adjuster

A Prayer for you...

Dear Reader,
I am a believer in God and in prayer. The Bible teaches that God is "a present help in the time of trouble." Many times, while helping a person with a loss and handling a claim, I have not been certain what action to take. It is during those times that I slow down, then pause and pray. I ask God for wisdom. Inevitably, soon thereafter, I will find the solution. It may come in a new thought, greater peace and less anxiety, a conversation with a person, or some new discovery found through closer observation or research. Sometimes I see the minds of decision makers change, sometimes it is my own mind that changes, but, one thing is certain...I am better off for having prayed.

May I Pray for you?
"God in heaven, you are good and nothing takes you by surprise. You are available and listening. I ask for the reader of this book, and whoever has experienced a loss...that you would give them peace and direction and guidance. I ask that you would guide them, and that their family would be encouraged. I ask that you would strengthen them through wise counsel and that you would surround them with others that might encourage and strengthen them. May they not feel alone, but supported.
I ask this in the name of your son, Amen."

Please feel free to email me at Rick@howtosettleyourclaim.com

Addendum

Contents

Name

Property Address

Item #	Room	Description	Age	Manufacturer serial #	Price	Photo #

Name:
Property Address:
Phone #:C.   W.
Begin at the front of your property and work your way around, checking off any damages.

Exterior Damaged Areas	Front	Right	Left	Rear
Roof				
Roof material is:				
Roof life expect.				
Roof trusses				
Decking (material under roof)				
Chimney				
Skylights				
Drip edge (metal edge of roofing)				
Flashing (metal in roof valleys or edge)				
Ridge vent				
Vents				
Rain gutters				
Down spouts				
Soffitt (area up under edge of roof)				
Fascia				
Masonry damage				
Vinyl or aluminum siding				
Wood damage				
Window damage: Type of window:				
Shutters				
Awnings				
Door damage				
Sliding glass doors: Other:				
Porch damage				
Fan damage				
Exterior light				
Exterior electrical				
Air conditioning				
Other:				
Other Structures				
Deck				
Pool				
Pool enclosure				
Fence				
Gazebo				
Other:				
Landscaping				
Tree Type:( ) Num(				
Tree Type:( ) Num(				
Shrubbery Type:				

www.RLCarterAdjuster.com

135

Name:
Property Address:
Phone # C.   W.
Beginning at your entry, look at the ceiling and proceed to walls and floor. Check off all damages in each room.

Interior Damaged Areas	Entry	Living	Dining	Family	Den	Breakf.
Attic						
Ceiling insulation						
Ceiling lights						
Ceiling fan						
AC/Heat vents						
Ceiling: mater. ( )						
Crown molding						
Walls						
Wall insulation						
Wallpaper						
Paneling						
Window treatments						
Electrical outlets						
Door and trim						
Window trim						
Chair rail						
Baseboard						
Shoe molding						
Wood floor						
Carpet						
Tile						
Vinyl flooring						
Sub floor						
Other:						
Other:						
Other:						
Other:						

www.RLCarterAdjuster.com

Name:
Property Address:
Phone #: C.   W.
Begin at the ceiling, then proceed to walls and floors. Check off damages

Interior Damaged Areas	M. Bed	Bed 1	Bed 2	Bed 3	Hall 1	Hall 2
Attic						
Ceiling insulation						
Ceiling lights						
Ceiling fan						
AC/Heat vents						
Ceiling: mater. ( )						
Crown molding						
Walls						
Wall insulation						
Wallpaper						
Paneling						
Window treatments						
Electrical outlets						
Door and trim						
Window trim						
Chair rail						
Baseboard						
Shoe molding						
Wood floor						
Carpet						
Tile						
Vinyl flooring						
Sub floor						
Other:						
Other:						
Other:						
Other:						

www.RLCarterAdjuster.com

Name:
Property Address:
Phone #: C.   W.
Begin at ceiling and proceed to walls and floors. Look inside cabinets to check walls. Note all damages.

Interior Damaged Areas	Kitchen	Pantry	Utility	Laundry	Garage	Basement
Attic						
Ceiling insulation						
Ceiling lights						
Ceiling fan						
AC/Heat vents						
Ceiling: Mater.						
Crown molding						
Walls						
Wall insulation						
Wallpaper						
Outlets						
Paneling						
Whdow treatments						
Electrical outlets						
Door and trim						
Window trim						
Chair rail						
Lower cabinets						
Upper cabinets						
Countertop						
Tub tile						
Tub faucets						
Sink						
Shower tile						
Mirror						
Baseboard						
Shoe molding						
Wood floor						
Carpet						
Tile						
Vinyl flooring						
Sub floor						
Exhaust vent						
Garbage disposal						
Dishwasher						
Refrigerator						
Washer						
Other:						
Other:						

Name:
Property Address:
Phone #: C.   W.
Begin at ceiling and proceed down walls to floor. Check off damages.

Interior Damaged Areas	M. Bath	Bath 1	Bath 2	1/2 Bath	Other
Attic					
Ceiling insulation					
Ceiling lights					
Ceiling fan					
AC/Heat vents					
Ceiling: mater. ( )					
Crown molding					
Walls					
Wall insulation					
Wallpaper					
Outlets					
Paneling					
Window treatments					
Electrical outlets					
Door and trim					
Window trim					
Chair rail					
Lower cabinets					
Upper cabinets					
Countertop					
Tub tile					
Tub faucets					
Sink					
Shower tile					
Mirror					
Baseboard					
Shoe molding					
Wood floor					
Carpet					
Tile					
Vinyl flooring					
Sub floor					
Other:					
Other:					
Other:					
Other: